IMAGES
of America

STAFFORD

ON THE COVER: This photograph shows the start of the 1919 Memorial Day parade. The marchers assembled at the Stafford Library and proceeded onto Spring Street. They are shown crossing the Christopher Allen Bridge on their way to the Stafford Springs Cemetery. The parade was led by the Phoenix Liberty Band, followed by veterans of World War I, the Spanish-American War, and the Civil War, and members of the Woman's Relief Corp. (Courtesy of the Stafford Historical Society.)

IMAGES
of America

STAFFORD

Rebecca Stocking Kraussmann
for the Stafford Historical Society

A

ARCADIA
PUBLISHING

Published by Arcadia Publishing
Charleston, South Carolina

Printed in the United States of America

Library of Congress Control Number: 2019941205

For all general information, please contact Arcadia Publishing:
Telephone 843-853-2070
Fax 843-853-0044
E-mail sales@arcadiapublishing.com
For customer service and orders:
Toll-Free 1-888-313-2665

Visit us on the Internet at www.arcadiapublishing.com

This book is in memory of Mike Hayden, Stafford Historical Society member and dedicated volunteer. His wit, compassion, and ability to fix everything are deeply missed.

CONTENTS

ACKNOWLEDGMENTS

This book would never have been written if it weren't for the assistance of several people who share my passion for Stafford history. David and Jean Bartlett, president and treasurer, respectively, of the Stafford Historical Society, were with me every step of the way on this journey. Dave wrote the introduction and many captions as well as helping me when I got stuck and reading everything I wrote. His knowledge of Stafford history is much greater than mine, so he was a resource as well as a collaborator. Jean proofread the book, lending her skills as an English teacher. Beth Magura, a retired editor, lent her magic as a professional copy-reader, not only asking questions and making suggestions but also tweaking my verbiage, which made the book better. Marc Nevue did research and was always prepared to search through newspapers to find some answer or fact that I was looking for.

Thank you to the Connecticut State Library for choosing to digitize the *Stafford Press* for Chronicling America in 2018. Much of our research was done in old newspapers, and having this resource for 1883–1922 online allowed me to find details that make this book more interesting. Other resources that I used were the publications of Bruce Dutton and William McDermott. Thank you to Lou DeSantis and Paul Burns for lending me photographs from your collections. Also, thank you to Arcadia Publishing for the Images of America series. My desire to have Stafford represented in this series spurred me on to do this project.

And, lastly, thank you to my family—Chuck, Katie, Aaron, and Scarlett—for putting up with me while I wrote this book.

All images in this volume appear courtesy of the Stafford Historical Society, unless otherwise noted.

INTRODUCTION

Founded in 1719, the town of Stafford is celebrating 300 years of a long and rich history. In the 1700s, Stafford was primarily an agricultural community. Starting in the 1800s, and lasting well into the 1900s, it developed into a center of manufacturing. This constant process of transformation continues to shape the town to the present day.

In 1718, the Colony of Connecticut appointed a surveyor to lay out the town. He chose a high, flat region in the northeast section for the initial settlement. The first street, originally called Broad Street, is what we now know as Stafford Street. The adjacent land was divided into 200-acre building lots, which were sold to the original settlers. Each landowner was required to build a dwelling upon his land within two years. Most of the early colonists remained within the Broad Street area, but some chose to locate in the outlying districts, becoming the first inhabitants of the future villages of Stafford Hollow, Hydeville, Staffordville, Orcuttville, West Stafford, and Stafford Springs.

The small settlement on Broad Street showed steady growth throughout the early 1700s. A meetinghouse was built, and the first parish was organized under the leadership of Rev. John Graham. A second wave of hardy settlers arrived, significantly expanding the population of the town. The first gristmills and sawmills were put into operation along the abundant waterways, which provided the power for the machinery.

Stafford's industrial history had its true beginning in the 1730s, when local entrepreneurs tapped the natural iron ore deposits in area bogs. They established an ironworks in Furnace Hollow, now called Stafford Hollow. Several other iron forges followed in succeeding years. By 1840, the supply of iron ore had been depleted, and large-scale iron production was no longer sustainable.

Despite the decline of the iron industry locally, the same iron ore deposits that had provided the basic raw material for so long remained a major catalyst of Stafford's economy for many years. Stafford's famed mineral waters were the direct result of the ore deposits. The many benefits of consuming and bathing in the water were well known to the Native Americans, who referred to the site of today's village of Stafford Springs as Medicine Springs. As early as 1765, newspaper accounts touted the curative effects of the water. At the same time, its medicinal qualities were being endorsed by physicians from as far away as Boston and New York City.

The extensive publicity resulted in a steady flow of visitors from near and far, journeying to Stafford in hopes of experiencing the healing properties of the water. The continuous stream of colonial health-seekers—including, in 1771, future president of the United States John Adams—earned Stafford Springs its designation as the nation's first resort. In 1802, to accommodate the influx of visitors, Dr. Samuel Willard built the first Stafford Springs House adjacent to the spring. With an ever-increasing number of patrons, Dr. Willard doubled the size of his hotel in 1812.

During the early and mid-1800s, Stafford remained primarily an agricultural community. Raising cattle and sheep were the most common types of farming, as the rugged terrain and rocky soil made cultivating crops difficult. However, by the 1840s, the impact of the Industrial Revolution had reached Stafford, laying the basis for subsequent decades of prosperity.

Sizeable factories were built along the many waterways throughout town, most of them producing textiles such as satinets or woolen fabric. Each of Stafford's six major villages is the direct result of one or more thriving factories operating nearby. The same can also be said of the smaller and lesser-known mill villages of Forestville, Foxville, and Glynville.

Each factory promoted the nearby development and growth of many smaller support industries, such as machine shops, sawmills, and blacksmith shops. Suitable housing for workers was also built within walking distance of the mills. Stores and shops, often owned by the factory owners, were opened to meet the everyday domestic needs of the employees. As Stafford prospered, numerous churches and schools were built throughout town to satisfy the religious and educational needs of the growing population. Throughout the remainder of the 1800s and well into the early 1900s, the individual mill villages functioned somewhat independently, each one capable of providing its inhabitants the basic necessities for a comfortable existence.

One of the most significant events in the history of Stafford occurred in March 1850. It was then that the northern extension of the New London, Willimantic & Palmer Railroad reached Stafford Springs. At long last, there was an efficient and economical means of transporting passengers and goods in and out of Stafford. Local industries received a tremendous boost, as manufacturers could more easily bring in raw materials and ship out their finished products. Merchants and shopkeepers offered a wider and more diverse selection of wares and articles in their stores than had been previously possible.

In March 1877, after a severe storm, the dam of the Staffordville reservoir burst. The ensuing flood surged downstream, destroying buildings and more dams in its path. When the 20-foot-high wall of water reached downtown Stafford Springs, it swept away houses, stores, the Stafford Springs Congregational Church, the Stafford National Bank, and many other buildings. Despite the extraordinary devastation, Stafford recovered and rebuilt, stronger than ever, paving the way for the commercial and industrial prosperity that lasted well into the 1900s.

Stafford experienced significant growth in its population during the late 1800s and early 1900s. Irish, German, Italian, Czech, Slovak, and French Canadian immigrants arrived in large numbers, seeking employment in the flourishing textile plants. Each nationality left its unique mark on Stafford through social organizations, businesses, churches, and more. During the same time, Stafford was also the recipient of significant bequests from several generous benefactors, including the Charles Holt Fountain, Hyde Park, the Christopher Allen Bridge, the Stafford Public Library, the Cyril and Julia Johnson Memorial Hospital, and Warren Memorial Town Hall.

Stafford's overall prosperity mirrored that of many small New England mill towns. The economic success or failure of the town was directly linked to that of the textile mills. After World War II, the textile industry had shifted largely to the southern states, eliminating many local jobs. Stafford residents took jobs in neighboring towns or in nearby cities, such as Willimantic, Hartford, or Springfield. The era of the commuter began, and Stafford became a "bedroom community."

Since the early 1960s, there has been a gradual shift in the business district from Main Street to Route 190 and the Shopper's Plaza in West Stafford. In recent times, however, many small businesses have again appeared on Main Street, which has also become a center for the arts and entertainment.

For 300 years, through good times and bad, whether celebrating achievements or dealing with adversities, Stafford has endured and prospered. We are grateful to all those who came before us and are a part of this history. It is our duty to continue to record and preserve our history for the benefit of future generations.

One

STAFFORD SPRINGS

In 1719, the first street in Stafford was laid out on high, flat ground suitable for farming, which was the principal occupation of the first settlers. Today's Stafford Street—then called Broad Street—remained the center of town for many years. As industry developed in the nearby valleys to take advantage of abundant waterpower, people followed—first to the village of Furnace Hollow, and, by the 1870s, to Stafford Springs.

The village name commemorates the local iron and sulfur springs long enjoyed by the Native Americans, who camped here during annual migrations. News of the springs' restorative qualities spread, and colonists, including future president John Adams, journeyed to Stafford to enjoy the water's benefits. Visitors either drank the water or submerged their entire bodies in one of the several bathhouses adjacent to the springs. In 1802, a hotel was built near the springs, which, in various forms, became a fixture in the village for over 150 years. Despite the appeal of the mineral springs, even in the 1830s the village consisted of only a few houses and farms. In the next 20 years, however, a prospering settlement developed around three textile mills. By 1857, the village had a grocery store, dry goods dealer, physician, furniture builder, carpenter, blacksmith, wagonmaker, jeweler, tailor, butcher, bank, school, and church.

The arrival of the railroad in 1850 was the most important factor in establishing Stafford Springs as the economic center of the town. The railway provided not only passenger service but, more importantly, a means of conveying raw goods and manufactured products into and out of town. In 1873, Stafford Springs became a chartered borough. Municipal improvements spread gradually, such as macadamized roads and town water and sewer. The flourishing textile mills helped Stafford Springs become a modern, prosperous village, and the area continued growing well into the 20th century. The borough was dissolved in 1991.

Northwest view of Stafford Mineral Springs Hotel.

Built in 1802, the first hotel (shown above in an engraving dated 1837) accommodated guests hoping to restore their health with the spring's water, thus making this the nation's first spa. In the stereopticon image below, a hand pump is protected by the roofed structure in the foreground. Today, springwater still flows nonstop from a recessed pipe stained orange from the iron, nestled between the Stafford Historical Society Museum and Grace Episcopal Church, both built years after this scene. Probably photographed on Memorial Day 1873, the parade was led by the Stafford Torrent Engine Fire Company, which is assembled on the bridge. The parade had returned from visiting all the cemeteries and is heading south on Spring Street to the Springs House to hear a Memorial Day speech.

By 1812, business at the mineral springs had prospered and the hotel's size was doubled, as shown here in a c. 1893 photograph. This building was torn down to make way for a new Stafford Springs House, which opened in 1896 but was lost to fire in 1959. It sat at the crest of the hill on Spring Street at the location of today's Hobbs Medical parking lot.

This pre-1877 view of Stafford Springs faces west from East Main Street toward Main Street. At left is the imposing Stafford National Bank building, which also housed the offices of the Stafford Savings Bank. Built in 1850, the Stafford Springs Congregational Church is at right. Both structures were destroyed by the flood of 1877 that devastated the downtown area.

Dated between 1868 and 1877, this northward view from Highland Terrace includes what is now Hyde Park and, beyond Middle River, the Mineral Springs Manufacturing Company, owned by the Converse family. On the hill are the spires of the First United Methodist Church (left) and St. Edward the Confessor Church (right). Main Street is just behind the mill.

This 1886 view shows Woodlawn mansion, the home of Julius Converse, built in 1871. The mansion and grounds overlooked the Mineral Springs Manufacturing Company, also owned by Converse, who was a civic benefactor and was politically active at both the state and local levels. His elegant home burned in 1929, and the town's second high school was built there in 1938.

Behind Woodlawn was a pond used for fishing, canoeing, and harvesting ice during the winter. The estate was a working farm, complete with a large barn, an icehouse, and quarters for employees. Cleared hillsides behind the house were used as pastureland for the farm's prizewinning dairy cows.

In 1911, the Town of Stafford purchased the former Converse estate, Woodlawn, to establish a public park. This was made possible by a generous bequest from the estate of Isaac Perkins Hyde, a Stafford native who achieved success manufacturing knives and blades in Southbridge, Massachusetts. He endowed this magnificent gift, which was named in his honor, to his beloved hometown, where it is still enjoyed today.

By 1929, Woodlawn mansion, long-time centerpiece of Hyde Park, had fallen into disrepair. It was auctioned off for salvage, but within 12 hours was severely damaged by fire. This c. 1911 photograph shows a copse of pine trees that stood next to the mansion. A filigreed gazebo once stood among the trees until it was destroyed in the hurricane of 1938.

In 1912, Christopher Allen, a local businessman and bank officer, funded construction of a new stone bridge to give Hyde Park the grand entrance it deserved. It took 1,600 tons of granite quarried in Monson, Massachusetts, and 35 tons of cement to build this sturdy bridge. Outfitted with elegant electric streetlights atop molded cast-iron poles, the bridge is still a beautiful part of downtown Stafford.

14

The c. 1912 photograph above shows an iconic view of Hyde Park and Woodlawn in the distance, the Christopher Allen Bridge, and the old Stafford Library. At right, the Stafford Library is seen from the north bank of Middle River. It was built in 1889 by Julius Converse as his office for the Mineral Springs Manufacturing Company and for the bottling works of the Stafford Springs Mineral Water Company. Upon Converse's death, Julia Johnson, wife of textile magnate Cyril Johnson, purchased the property from the estate, and in 1896, deeded it to the Stafford Library Association. The first library in town opened in 1877, using borrowed space on Main Street. The library relocated several times until the donation of this architecturally unique building.

Details of the original interior of the library that date from 1896, such as the woodwork and ceiling, can still be seen today by visiting the Stafford Historical Society Museum, which keeps its collections here. More than a century of service as a library ended in 2001, when the new public library opened in the multi-school complex on Levinthal Run.

The Holt Memorial Fountain in Haymarket Square was erected in 1894 in memory of mill owner Charles Holt by his wife and daughter. The urns were watering troughs for animals, and a nearby spigot allowed people to drink from the fountain, too. Originally, a glass globe above the central fountain contained small, colored glass balls that danced around inside the globe on the piped-in water.

With the Congregational church and Cyril Johnson's woolen mill as backdrop, a one-horsepower buggy has pulled up to the Holt Memorial Fountain around 1900. From 1939 to 1997, no water ran in the fountain, but a public campaign succeeded in getting water flowing again. In 1990, relocation of the fountain to improve modern traffic flow was considered, but the town rejected it.

Stafford's first town hall, built in 1845, was unheated and located in Stafford Hollow. In 1873, the municipality became a borough, and town offices were added upstairs in a new fire house on River Road. In 1920, Col. Charles Warren, a local businessman and Civil War veteran, left money expressly for a new town hall. In 1923, the Warren Memorial Town Hall was completed in Haymarket Square.

The c. 1890 view above looks east down Main Street toward Haymarket Square. The buildings on the right still stand in 2019, joined by others over the years. The L. Helm Dry Goods store, at left, is where the Palace Theatre is today, just west of Fiske Avenue. Below, this c. 1910 view farther down Main Street captures a Connecticut Company trolley car rumbling along. Trolley service between Stafford and Rockville began in 1908 and lasted until 1928. The Baker Block, visible directly behind the trolley car, housed several businesses. Most prominent was G.H. Baker & Co., a home furnishings store that was one of the earliest businesses in Stafford, founded in 1808. In 1917, a fire destroyed the Baker Block. This is the current site of Warren Memorial Town Hall.

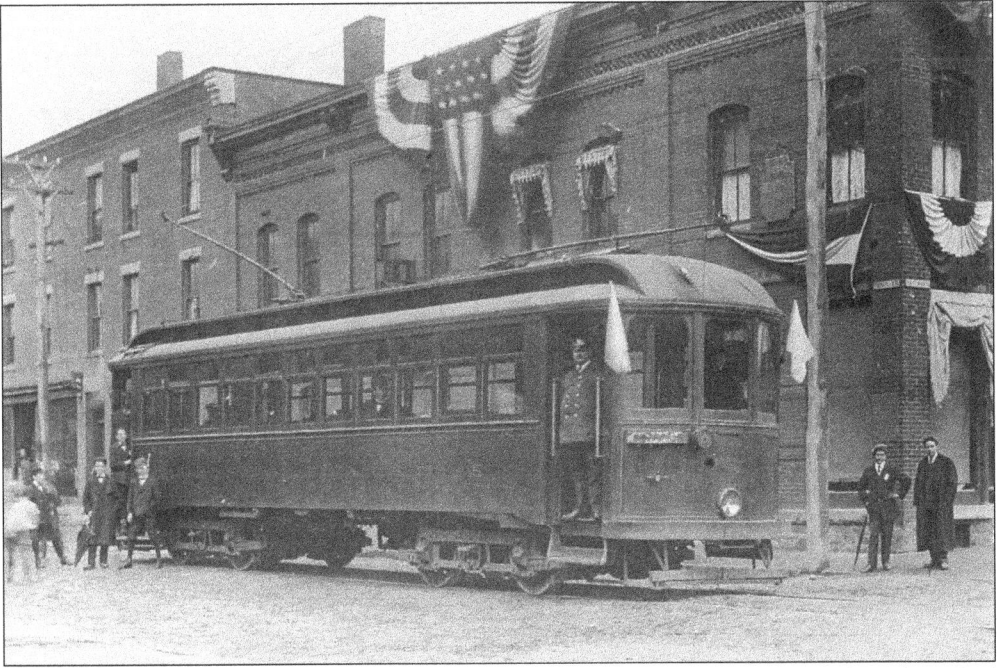

April 20, 1908, was the long-anticipated first day of trolley service between Rockville and Stafford Springs. The passenger fare for the 30-minute trip was 15¢. Above, a trolley car is stopped at the intersection of East Main Street and Furnace Avenue, a short distance from where the trolley terminal still stands in 2019. It was a day of town-wide celebration, with mills, businesses, and schools closed for the occasion. Buildings were adorned with decorative bunting, and festivities included a parade, speeches, band concerts, a baseball game, and a fireworks display. Below, on May 1, 1928, the last trolley to travel on Main Street coexisted with motorized vehicles, a horse-drawn wagon, and the railroad.

Levi Gary, local liveryman and teamster, waits at the railroad station for the train that brought the town's mail. For nearly 40 years, he and his gray mare, Dobbin, delivered the mail to the post office, three times daily. This ended in 1939 when the post office awarded the contract to the owner of a motorized truck, who was able to underbid Gary.

Built in 1893, the Central Vermont Railway passenger station replaced an earlier one located at the corner of Main and Spring Streets. A covered passenger platform extended beyond the building but was removed in the 1930s. Architecturally noteworthy are the original eyebrow windows on the south side of the station roof. The Stafford Police and resident state trooper are based here in 2019.

Train accidents and derailments were not uncommon, although some were more dramatic than others. On March 2, 1905, Engine No. 329 derailed near the Smith & Cooley mill. It took several days to raise it back onto the track. This curve is the tightest turn on the entire 121-mile route of the Southern Division of the Central Vermont Railway between New London, Connecticut, and Brattleboro, Vermont. Willington Avenue runs parallel to the tracks behind the train, and Westford Avenue intersects. The three-story building on the hill was the Boys' Club and is now apartments. The E.C. Dennis Grain Mill, with the tall chimney, is on the corner of Willington and Westford Avenues. The gable end of the CVR freight house is visible to the right. Engine No. 329 derailed two more times in the next year and a half, leading to one newspaper's description of its exploits as a "shadowy past."

This c. 1900 panoramic photograph is of East Main Street near the intersection of Crown Street. From the 1870s into the first two decades of the 1900s, many stately homes were built by mill owners and businessmen on East Main Street, Edgewood Street, and Highland Terrace. Several older houses on East Main Street were torn down to make way for these modern manses, including the small house on the left. This was the home of Francis N. Crane, leather dealer and harness maker. Following his death in 1904, this lot was sold and a new, modern house was built in its place. The elaborate barn for the Christopher Allen house can be seen in the background on

the right. The second home on the left was built by Christopher Allen, one of the owners of the Phoenix Mill in Hydeville, and benefactor of the Christopher Allen Bridge on Spring Street. The house on the right is at the corner of East Main and Crown Streets. This was built by William Smith, founder of the Smith & Cooley Company. Born in Stafford, Smith learned about the woolen business by working at the Charles Fox Company in Foxville. He was part owner of a mill in Stafford Hollow but sold that and started his own shoddy and flock mill in Stafford Springs. This is now the Introvigne Funeral Home.

The Parkess house at the intersection of Prospect, Parkess, and Church Streets is considered to be the oldest house in downtown Stafford. Aaron Parkess came to Stafford about 1790, establishing a farm and building this house. He also made scythes and nails. The house is largely unchanged today.

This 1935 photograph is of the Charles Holt Homestead on East Main Street. Holt was born in Willington in 1827, but moved to Stafford to apprentice in a machine shop, eventually becoming its superintendent. He next accepted the position of superintendent of the Phoenix Woolen Company in Hydeville, where he ultimately became the sole owner. Holt lived in this house with his wife, Joanna, and their daughter Celia.

Two

THE VILLAGES

Before the mill villages started to grow, Stafford's original settlements were on Stafford Street and on today's Hampden Road in West Stafford. Both locations were flat and on the top of a hill, making them more suitable for farming. At the turn of the 19th century, most people were living in one of these areas, with almost 40 percent of Stafford's residents living in West Stafford in 1796.

Stafford Street was laid out as the center of town, with large house lots next to each other. The street was 110 yards wide, more than the length of a football field. A church, a schoolhouse, and a cemetery were built to accommodate the needs of the residents. The hilltop settlement of West Stafford also had its own church and cemetery. By the mid-1800s, small industry had started to develop along the numerous brooks and streams in the valley. There were a few small mills over the years, but most manufacturing involved machine shops, many owned and operated by innovative and creative craftsmen. More major patents were granted to inventors in West Stafford than in any other village in Stafford. In 1854, due to the shift of the population into the valley, the decision was made to move the Second Congregational Church from the top of the hill down Hampden Road to its present location. This task was accomplished by using a team of oxen pulling the building on wooden rollers. Stafford Hollow, also known as Furnace Hollow, started to grow when iron ore beds were discovered. John Phelps built a furnace and foundry in 1779 and started supplying cannons and cannonballs for the American Revolution. There were also small iron industries in Staffordville and Hydeville.

Stafford Hollow, Staffordville, and West Stafford were the biggest villages, because all had more than one mill; Hydeville, Orcuttville, and Foxville each had one mill and remained small.

The Miner Grant General Store on Stafford Street stocked everything a person of the day needed. The store was built around 1802 by Miner Grant Sr., replacing an earlier store built by Samuel Willard. It remained a store in the Grant family for over 100 years, closing in 1911. In 1938, Old Sturbridge Village moved the building and today uses it as a general store. (Courtesy of Louis DeSantis.)

This historic house, located on Stafford Street, was built around 1810 by Miner Grant, owner of the famed Miner Grant General Store. It is a superb example of Georgian architecture with its classical proportion, symmetrical arrangement of doors and windows, hip roof, and columned pediment over the front entryway. It is still owned by a great-great-great grandson of the original owner.

26

This Colonial-style home, located on Stafford Street, was built in 1790 by Rev. John Willard. For 50 years, Reverend Willard served as minister of the Stafford Street Congregational Church. He was a graduate of Harvard College and a classmate and personal friend of John Adams. His youngest son, Dr. Samuel Willard, built and owned the first Stafford Springs House in 1802. (Courtesy of Patricia Greika.)

Located at the intersection of Stafford Street and today's Crooked S Road, the Hyde Tavern featured an elegant ballroom on the second floor. In 1824, the Marquis de Lafayette, the last surviving French general of the Revolutionary War, spent a day at the tavern, receiving visitors during his nationwide farewell tour. Hyde Tavern was damaged by fire in 1961 and was later demolished. (Courtesy of Paul Burns.)

This c. 1895 photograph of Stafford Hollow shows Mill Pond and the Riverside Mill, built in 1881. In the 1830s, Jasper Hyde and Eli Horton built a textile mill on this same site. The buildings around the pond were built for laborers in the Riverside Mill or Valley Company Mill, which had been located at the north end of the pond. The latter mill burned in 1874 and was not rebuilt.

This postcard shows the bridge over the Mill Pond Dam. The view looks south toward the center of Stafford Hollow, where Orcuttville Road and East Street intersect. The Furnace Hollow Hotel, with its four columns, was at the corner of East Street and Patten Road until it was demolished in 1919. Several stores were clustered here as well as a carriage maker, post office, and saloon.

Located in the center of Stafford Hollow, these two buildings stood on the south end of Mill Pond. The building on the right is today's Millpond Country Store. Dating to 1845, it has housed many businesses over the years. Jacob Glover's Stove and Tin Shop is at the left. Both buildings housed the post office at various times. Wightman's carriage shop is in the background on the right.

The Old Town House, built in 1845, was the first nonsecular meeting place for residents. Previously, town meetings occurred at the meetinghouse on Stafford Street. But by 1845, the Hollow was the political center of the town. All town records were kept here until the Warren Memorial Town Hall was built in Stafford Springs in 1922–1923. Events such as roller-skating and silent movies were held here in the late 1800s.

In 1870, the A.C. Corpe machine shop (right) and foundry (left) was one of two foundries that remained in Stafford. Beyond is the home of Jarvis Hyde, on the left going up the hill, and Mrs. Hyde is at the door. The Hyde home was on Steep Gutter Road (now called Sunset Ridge), where it intersects with Old Monson Road.

In 1867, the Harmonial Progressive Union built a church in the center of Stafford Hollow. More commonly known as Spiritualists, this loosely organized religion believed in communication with the dead. Members also tended to support abolition and women's suffrage. The building was given to the town in 1900 for use as a community hall. The Baker family is gathered here on July 4, 1914, for a family reunion.

The old Edson homestead on Murphy Road in Stafford Hollow, shown in 1908, is the oldest house in Stafford Hollow, possibly dating to 1720. This was the home of John Phelps, who built the iron industry in the Hollow. Phelps Furnace stood nearby, where the Universalist church is today. In 2019, the house appears nearly unchanged.

Ephraim H. Hyde lived in this Murphy Road home. Hyde was a leader in agriculture, serving on many agricultural society boards and as a trustee of the Connecticut Agricultural School. He was a founder of the Stafford Fair and the state's 33rd lieutenant governor. This building has been demolished. Grace O. Chapman (on horse) and Rev. Leonard S. Goodell and his wife stand in front of the house. (Courtesy of Esther DaRos.)

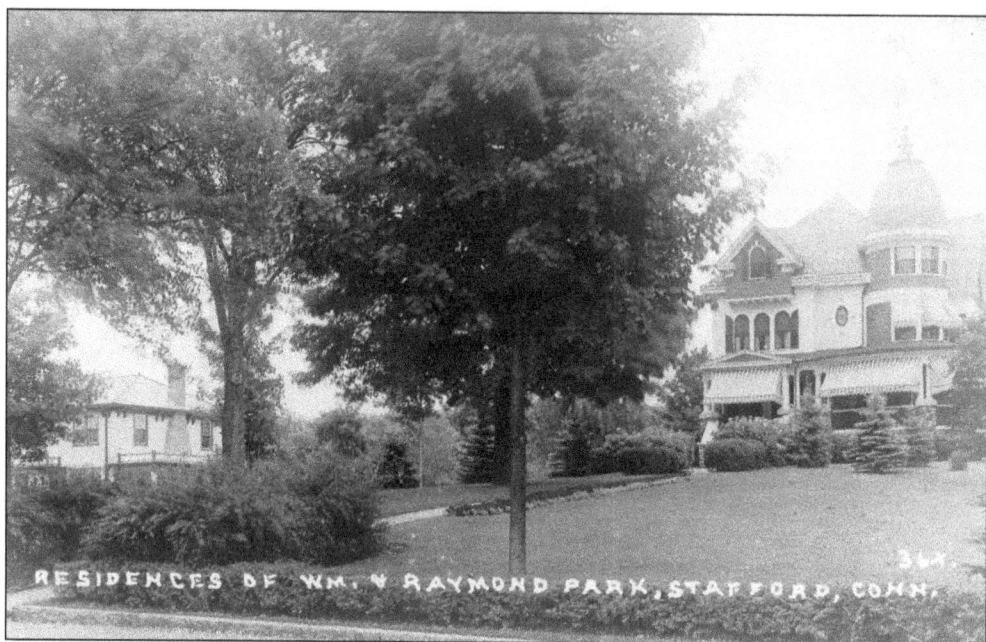

RESIDENCES OF WM. W RAYMOND PARK, STAFFORD, CONN.

The ornate Queen Anne–style residence on the right was built around 1890 by Alfred and Philena Preble. Alfred's occupation was a wheelwright. The house was later owned by William Park, who purchased the nearby Riverside Woolen in 1906. Park also acquired the adjacent lot and built the home seen on the left. This house became the residence of his son Raymond Park.

The stretch of land along West Stafford Road in the center of West Stafford was known as "the narrows." Industry grew here because of the streams, and the population moved here from Hampden Hill as the manufacturing industry became established. This undated view of the village looks northeast toward Orcuttville. The Bradway Grist Mill faces the road on the left, and Edson Brook runs through the meadow.

Bradway Falls on Edson Brook was near the intersection of Hampden and West Stafford Roads. The pond and dam were dynamited after the 1938 flood; today, only the brook remains. The building on the right was home to Bradway Grist Mill, Bradway Grains, the Bradway Filling Station, and later Mac's Drive-In, which was a favorite hangout for teenagers in the 1950s and 1960s.

In this view looking northwest from Murry Hill, the spire of the Second Congregational Church in West Stafford is visible on the left. Trolley tracks pass in the foreground, and a small station awaits riders. The large house on the right, seen from the back, was a tavern for many years. Owners included the Fairfield, Lewis, and Fairman families. Today, it is an apartment building.

This gas station stood at the corner of Routes 30 and 190, across from the Second Congregational Church in West Stafford. Today, these roads are not major thoroughfares, but before 1943, when the Wilbur Cross Highway was built, a person traveling from Hartford to Boston would go through this intersection. Today, this building is a house and is set back from the road.

The major geographic feature of Staffordville is the lake, which covers over 149 acres. This view was taken from Stafford Street looking toward the village. Staffordville's growth was triggered by the discovery of iron ore around 1801; a blast furnace was built near the present site of the dam. The village was often referred to as New Furnace. At one time, Staffordville was home to four textile mills.

This early view of Staffordville shows the thriving village. The Methodist church is visible at lower left, and the steeple of the Congregational church can be seen on the right. Colburn Road runs to the north, parallel to the lake. The Ruggles pistol factory was at the intersection of Colburn and Upper Roads, near the present site of the Staffordville Fire Department.

Lyons Road in Staffordville is considered by some to be the "Main Street" of the village. In 1897, fire broke out in the O'Dell & Jones general store and post office at this site. The store was destroyed, along with two houses, two barns, a barbershop, and a shoe shop. Pictured here is the Phelps and Cunningham store and post office, which replaced the burned store.

These two photographs are of the home and family of William Tobin, who lived on the corner of Upper Road and Route 19 in Staffordville. Tobin was born in Ireland during the Great Famine. He immigrated to the United States as a young child and came to Stafford before 1880. He was an iron molder by profession and probably worked at Amadon's Machine Shop in Staffordville. Below is the Tobin family. From left to right are Betsey (mother), Annie, Lizzie, William (father), James, and William Jr. sitting next to the easel. Note the Victorian interior with wallpaper on the ceiling and walls, a patterned carpet, and patterned curtains. H.C. Thresher , a prolific local photographer, took these photographs using glass negatives about 1895. The Stafford Historical Society has the negatives in its collection.

In 1855, the Staffordville Savings Bank was organized and located in this building on Lyons Road. In 1872, the bank charter was withdrawn and the bank was dissolved. Shortly thereafter, it was converted into a private home and remains so today. At the time of this c. 1910 photograph, it was owned by T.M. Lyon, who also operated the general store directly across the street.

This view of Staffordville shows East Street winding around the southernmost point of the lake. The intersection of Wales Road and New City Road is off to the left. The building on the far right with the large cupola is the old Staffordville schoolhouse, now a residence. This part of the lake used to be farmland, although when it was inundated is unknown.

Since 1850, the railroad has passed through Orcuttville, where passengers caught the train at the Orcutts station, shown here in the late 1920s. Orcutts was a whistle-stop station, meaning that the train only stopped if it was signaled to pick up a waiting passenger. Orcuttville remained a small village; in 1869, there was a woolen mill, a sawmill, and seven houses, some of which were used as tenements.

Gathered at the Orcutts station around 1911 are, from left to right, Alonzo Spellman (on the bicycle), the Smith sisters, William Bumstead, Cora Ford, Phebe Spellman, William Francis (conductor), and Jennie Spellman. Bumstead owned the Preble and Bumstead Box Factory in Orcuttville. He also served as a representative in the Connecticut General Assembly.

The village of Hydeville lies midway between Stafford Hollow and Staffordville. Lafayette Iron Furnace was built here in 1796 by Nathaniel Hyde and was later owned by Jasper Hyde. This foundry had the distinction of producing the first Connecticut-made stoves. Hydeville Mill, in the postcard above, was built in 1860 by Jarvis Hyde on the site of the old furnace. The village's population increased rapidly after 1868 when the Phoenix Woolen Company took over the mill and doubled production. Hydeville, like Orcuttville, was comprised mostly of tenement housing and one-family residences, since goods and services were easily accessible in nearby Stafford Hollow or Staffordville. The bird's-eye view below shows Hydeville in the early 1900s.

The village of Foxville, named for mill owner Charles Fox, is located along West and Center Streets. The railroad ran through the village, and the Foxville Mill could easily utilize the train for both shipping and receiving. This area was mainly residential, although the Stafford Fairgrounds are in this village. Its proximity to Stafford Springs allowed residents to easily walk downtown for all their basic needs.

An 1869 stereopticon shows the Charles Fox home on West Street, which still stands. In 1851, Fox purchased the Parley Converse Mill, renaming it the Charles Fox Company. Over the next 40 years, Fox erected new buildings and updated equipment, expanding the mill's production. During the Civil War, Foxville Mill was one of several Stafford textile mills that supplied fabric to the military.

Three

MILLS AND MANUFACTURING

Stafford's diverse geographic features—hills, valleys, and rivers—made the town a perfect location for water-powered mills. In the 1700s, there were a few sawmills and gristmills, but with the arrival of industrialization in the early 1800s, local entrepreneurs realized the potential of investing their money in the construction of textile mills. The mill owners also built tenement houses in which their employees could reside and company stores where they could shop. Villages started growing up around the mills as supporting industries, businesses, and laborers moved in.

Being a laborer in a textile mill was not easy, or safe, work. Generally, laborers worked 12 hours a day, six days a week. The air inside a mill was full of minute particles from fabric fibers, making it unhealthy to breathe. These fibers, as well as oil from the machines and the wool, combined to make a very flammable environment, frequently resulting in disastrous mill fires. Damaged or destroyed mills were generally rebuilt. Eventually, most large mills established their own fire departments. Staffordville boasted four textile mills, but only one was standing in 1886; the others had burned but were in the process of being rebuilt. The early mills were also susceptible to periodic shutdowns for various reasons. Water-powered mills were dependent on a steady, even flow of water. Periods of drought or excessive rain halted production, as did frozen streams or rivers. Also, mills often traded hands, sometimes experiencing a shutdown during the transition between owners. Additionally, the mills were subject to the prevailing economic conditions in the country. For example, all four textile mills in Staffordville were put up for sale during the Panic of 1873.

The textile industry was resilient, however, and continued growing despite all the difficulties that it faced. But, the introduction of man-made fibers, foreign competition, and the trend of mills moving south damaged the New England textile industry. The textile mills in Stafford started a slow but steady decline around 1950, and within 20 years, many of them had closed.

The Mineral Springs Manufacturing Company stood between Main Street and what would become Hyde Park. Built in 1839 by Solva Converse, this was the first textile mill in the village of Stafford Springs. Julius Converse, son of Solva, became sole owner of the property in 1885. His mansion, Woodlawn, overlooked the mill. In 1899, the mill changed hands and became the Faulkner Mill, which was destroyed by fire in 1913. The two spires along the tree line in the view above are the First United Methodist Church (left) and the first Stafford High School, located on High Street. Below are the burned ruins of the Faulkner Mill, dated 1913. In the foreground, a baseball game is being played in the new Hyde Park.

In 1916, the Stafford Worsted Company built a factory on the site of the old Faulkner Mill. Stafford Worsted, which had operated on Furnace Avenue from 1897 to 1910, produced a fine wool yarn that was woven into cloth in Rhode Island. In 1941, the mill had 200 employees, mostly women, and was the first in town to get a government contract for military fabric in World War II. The mill shut down in 1957. The same year, Linatex, which produced mechanical rubber products, purchased the building and was in business until 1991. In 1994, American Sleeve Bearing, manufacturer of bronze bushings and bearings, purchased the company and is still in business today. This photograph of Stafford Worsted Company was taken from Spring Street. Hyde Park is on the left, and the name is spelled out in white rocks above the band shell. Woodlawn is to the left.

In 1841, Ephraim Hyde built a cotton mill at the corner of what would become Furnace Avenue and East Main Street. Sold in 1843, the mill operated as the Granite Mill Company for the next 40 years. In 1888, the Central Woolen Company assumed ownership, converting the mill to the production of woolens. Cyril Johnson purchased the mill in 1907. Above is the original granite mill with the gabled end facing the camera and the brick Central Woolen office facing Furnace Avenue; the brick ell, built in 1890, was torn down in 1922. Today, Stafford Savings Bank stands next to the old granite part of the mill. Below is the original mill with recent additions. Today, the American Woolen Company offices are in the building facing Furnace Avenue.

From 1911 to 1963, the Cyril Johnson Mill was owned by the Mitchell family. Hale Manufacturing Company bought the mill in 1963 and began manufacturing nylon upholstery fabric. Warren Woolen purchased the mill in 1984. Here, an aerial view shows the Johnson Mill running along Furnace Avenue to High Street. Stafford Savings Bank is at lower left, with mill buildings behind it. Note the water tower.

Converseville Mill was built in 1853 by Parley Converse and brothers along with Benjamin and Robbins Patten. They brought highly skilled weavers from Yorkshire, England, and became renowned for producing high-quality woolens. In 1879, Daniel and Thomas Warren purchased the business, renaming it Warren Woolen Company. The four-story granite building with gabled end facing Furnace Avenue is part of the original 1853 structure, shown here between 1921 and 1930.

In 1890, Joseph M. Valentine purchased Warren Woolen and continued production of high-end wool. In 1992, Loro Piana of Italy bought the complex, including the old Johnson Mill. Loro Piana discontinued the Johnson Mill's upholstery line to focus on the cashmere and camel hair fabric that had made Warren Woolen famous. In 2013, American Woolen Company bought out Loro Piana, and as of 2019 is one of the few luxury wool manufacturers in the United States. Above, viewed from Silver Street, Warren Woolen sprawls out along Furnace Avenue. The view below is looking west across the Warren pond dam toward the mill. An 1883 brick addition is nearest the dam. The cupola and fancy brickwork in the gable and cornice were removed.

Glynville Mill was built about 1858 by Moses Harvey. Situated on the pond above Warren Woolen, the mill took its name from its location on Glyn Road—today's Furnace Avenue. The mill is in the foreground; a house and two tenements beyond were mill worker housing. The housing still stands, while only the foundation of the mill remains visible from the road today.

In 1885, Glynville Mill was sold to Smith & Cooley Company, and it transitioned into a shoddy mill. Damaged by the 1955 flood, the mill was bought by Warren Woolen for its water rights in 1956. The Town of Stafford and Warren Woolen worked together to rent the mill to an industry that did not rely on water, but they were unsuccessful. The building was torn down in 1959.

Smith & Cooley also operated a waste and shoddy mill on River Road. Built in 1875, this mill processed woolen waste to be used by other industries or to be woven into rough fabric. In 1941, A.W. Dolge and Frank Leuthner purchased the business and continued activity until 2003. The complex now consists of apartments and businesses, as well as yoga, dance, and art studios.

Rawitser & Company owned four mills in Stafford, two on River Road, and two in Staffordville. The River Mill, pictured, burned in 1911. One section of the complex remains and is the home of Hyde Autoworks today. A second mill downriver is now 3M Manufacturing. The photograph was taken about 1900. The building on the right of the mill was the fire department and is now Shamrock Laundry.

Hydeville Mill was organized about 1838, and the building shown dates to about 1860. In 1868, it became the Phoenix Woolen Company. In 1934, the Swift River Woolen Company of Rhode Island purchased the building. In 1955, A.W. Dolge changed the operations to a shoddy mill, and it ran for 21 years, closing in 1976. Although the mill is still standing today, it has started to collapse.

Orcuttville Mill was built as a woolen mill by three Orcutt brothers in 1852. In 1869, the mill was purchased by Ellis, Converse & Company. Textile manufacturing was discontinued in 1933, and the mill remained empty for decades. A chicken farm used the building for a short time, but it was sold in 1958. Again, the building stood unused until it was destroyed by fire in 1979.

The Foxville Mill was built by Parley Converse in 1837. In 1851, Charles Fox, who lent the village his surname, purchased the mill and renamed it Charles Fox and Company. In 1907, the Rhode Island Worsted Company purchased the complex, expanded production, and became known for the Olympic line of menswear fabric. The company built a mill village of 15 houses with town water and sewer to rent to its employees. In 1954, Stafford Printers, known for its line of silk fabrics used in parachutes, acquired Rhode Island Worsted. This company went through several mergers, and at its peak, employed over 500 people. It closed in 1980. Above, West Street runs past the many mill buildings about 1915. Below is a view of the intersection of Center and West Streets in the 1920s.

Located by the Mill Pond dam, this site in Stafford Hollow has been home to an iron blast furnace, sawmill, machine shop, and satinet mill. The Riverside Mill was built in 1881 by Cyril Johnson and Edwin C. Pinney to manufacture cassimere, a soft, woolen fabric. In 1906, William Park, a Scotsman who had immigrated to America about 1871, purchased the mill and started producing fancy suitings, becoming a leader in fine quality wool for men's and women's clothing. Because of the decline in the US textile industry, the mill closed in 1959. In 1964, the building was purchased by the North American Printed Circuit Corporation. Several mergers over the last 50 years have expanded the business, and it is now part of TTM Technologies. TTM, currently one of Stafford's largest employers, has accurately preserved the historic character of the building. In 2014, TTM reconstructed a replica of the original cupola, which had been removed many years ago. The house shown on the right in this c. 1890 photograph was the home of Cyril and Julia Johnson. (Courtesy of Louis DeSantis.)

In 1839, the Staffordville Manufacturing Company was built at the corner of Route 19 and Colburn Road. The mill, which manufactured satinets, changed hands several times before being destroyed by fire in 1886. The mill was rebuilt and purchased by the Garland Woolen Company in 1899. This structure burned in 1914 and was not rebuilt. In this view from Stafford Street hill looking west, the mill is the four-story structure at center.

In 1852, Eliab A. Converse built the Hope Mill at the foot of Staffordville Dam, where an early iron foundry had been destroyed by fire in 1851. The Hope Mill burned and was rebuilt twice before 1886. In 1915, the building, shown here around 1925, was purchased by the United Pearl Button Company of New York, which produced buttons from exotic Pacific seashells.

In 1917, the button factory was conveyed to Benedict Schwanda and renamed B. Schwanda & Sons. Schwanda founded the business in 1882 in Czechoslovakia before immigrating to the United States. In 1927, a new brick factory, shown above, was built next to the original mill. In 1953, another addition was built, and the top three floors of the old mill were removed. In 1963, the company converted to manufacturing plastic buttons and became Schwanda Plastics, which closed in 1984. Today, this complex is one of three TTM Technologies locations in Stafford. In the 1940s aerial view below, the old four-story mill building is at left and the old Stafford No. 1 Fire Department is to the right of the 1927 building. Staffordville School is at upper right.

This view of West Stafford looks east across Crystal Lake Road (Route 30). The building to the left of Fly Pond, built about 1860, was used as a twine mill, machine shop, shoddy mill, and gun factory. In 1922, John Soukup, a Czechoslovakian immigrant, started producing mother-of-pearl novelties and buttons. The factory closed in 1957. The house to the right is still standing. The mill is abandoned today.

This view from Krol Road shows David E. Whiton's machine shop and house on West Stafford Road. From 1852 to 1888, he manufactured waterwheels and chucks. In 1889, Charles P. Bradway, maker of the Bradway turbine, purchased the mill. In World War I, Bradway had the largest vertical chuck in the state, so Pratt & Whitney sent aircraft engine parts via trolley for Bradway to mill. The trolley tracks crossed Krol Road.

Four

BUSINESSES

The history of businesses in Stafford is almost as old as the town itself. In the earliest days, most inhabitants were farmers, whose needs were simple and few. They generally were self-sufficient, producing everything from food to clothing to tools—or they went without. By the mid-18th century, however, specialty businesses sprang up to address the growing needs of the people. These included sawmills, gristmills, blacksmith shops, and harness shops. Other commercial businesses soon followed—general stores at first, followed by specialty stores such as tin shops, cabinetmakers, tailors, dry goods, household goods, and groceries. Each village had the essential businesses to meet the basic needs of everyday life.

The enduring fame of the mineral springs, along with the arrival of the railroad in 1850, transformed Stafford Springs into the town's commercial and business center, where nearly half of the population lived and worked. This increased population and the influx of visitors generated a broad selection of business establishments. Merchants and retailers sold everything from home-grown goods produced on local farms and in area shops and factories, to exotic items imported from around the world. People could buy anything they needed right in town. The types of businesses and the names of the merchants changed over the years, and business boomed until well after World War II. However, the decline of the woolen industry and the subsequent closing of the mills devastated Stafford's businesses. Long-established stores struggled to attract customers and either closed their doors or moved elsewhere. The empty storefronts on Main Street were an unkind reminder of difficult economic times and changing shopping preferences.

For the past decade, Main Street has been steadily experiencing revitalization. Attracted by the unique character of the remaining late 19th- and early 20th-century buildings, small shopkeepers, pub owners, artisans, and musicians are adding their own vibrancy to Main Street. The Stafford Garden Club has worked hard to maintain attractive gardens in the downtown. Also, increased civic involvement exemplifies the collaborative, community-minded spirit that, once invested, reaps positive change—step by step. Hopefully, this trend will continue well into the future.

In 1808, Henry C. Baker opened a cabinetry business on East Main Street, selling furniture and coffins. In 1851, his son Gilbert H. Baker built a store on Haymarket Square, shown here in 1879. Destroyed by fire in 1917, the business moved to Furnace Avenue. In 1964, Roger Rossi purchased Baker's Furniture and moved it to West Main Street, where his family operated it until 2015.

In 1889, Julius Converse's Stafford Springs Mineral Water Company began bottling the famed springwater at a new building on Spring Street, shown here. The water won a gold medal at the St. Louis World's Fair in 1904. James Campo ran the company from 1913 until 1934, when he switched to making soda. The renamed Stafford Ginger Ale Company operated on West Street until closing in 2003.

In 1855, the first bank in Stafford opened in the Granite Mill, incorporating in 1858 as the Savings Bank of Stafford Springs. The Stafford National Bank, shown here, was built in 1859 at the corner of East Main Street and Haymarket Square. By 1872, the Stafford Savings Bank had also set up offices in this building, which was destroyed in the flood of 1877.

In 1878, the new Stafford National Bank building, shown here, was erected on the site of the previous building. In 1888, the bank became the First National Bank of Stafford Springs. In 1948, the Hartford-Connecticut Trust Company remodeled this building by removing the third floor and modernizing all exterior details. In 1987, the building was owned by Connecticut Bank & Trust when fire destroyed it.

Incorporated in 1872, the Stafford Savings Bank later merged with the Savings Bank of Stafford Springs. In 1905, the bank moved from the First National Bank building into the Warren Block, shown in this image, at the corner of Main and Spring Streets. In 1928, Stafford Savings moved to a new building on Furnace Avenue. In 2019, the Stafford Coffee Company occupies this space along with the old bank vault.

Stafford Savings Bank outgrew the building on Main Street—in particular, because a larger vault was needed. A lot was purchased next to the Stafford Springs Congregational Church, where two tenements were demolished. Boston architectural firm Thomas M. James Company designed the brick-and-limestone exterior pictured here. The new location was occupied in 1928.

The William A. Comins Carriage Shop, shown above, opened in 1867 on Willington Avenue. Comins specialized in a two-seat Concord carriage but built all types of horse-drawn vehicles. This building was later used as Mattesen's Service Station and Shark Cycle, and is still standing. Gary Brothers Livery and Stables, shown below, was started about 1865 by Levi Gary and later run by his sons Charles B. and Dana Gary. It was located behind Comins Carriage Shop. Besides boarding and selling horses and supplies, they also sold coal, the major fuel of the time. Charles's son George ran the business until his death in 1928. The Gary Brothers wagon in the image below is probably a Comins carriage, offering rows of bench seating and weatherproof curtains—with "Stafford" painted on the sides.

The Italian Cooperative & Social Club was founded in 1911 by 40 Italian mill workers in Stafford. Membership was offered to local Italians, who could save money by buying food staples at wholesale prices. In 1921, the business was reorganized as the Worker's Cooperative Union, and membership was opened to anyone. Shown here is the interior of the first store on Main Street in 1922.

In 1928, a new Worker's Cooperative Union store was built on Main Street; it was remodeled in 1940. The second floor was used for meetings, a nursery school, and home extension classes. In 1943, the union members opened their own slaughterhouse, Home Pride. A new store on West Main was occupied in 1954 and was in business until 1989.

Built in 1915, the Bidorini building on Main Street had room for Alfred Bidorini's grocery store, on the right; William Benton's Lunch Room, in the middle; and the Panciera Saloon, on the left. Today, the Stafford Cidery occupies this building. There is still a large, built-in oven for baking bread in the basement. (Courtesy of Louis DeSantis.)

This 1909 photograph shows the Converse Block, built the year before. Among the first tenants were Frank Fitzpatrick, news dealer; John Leach, tailor and haberdasher; and Anders Jacobsen's pharmacy. The offices of Dr. Lucius Eaton and Dr. John Hanley were on the second floor. This building eventually became the McCormick Drug Store. In 2019, Rustology Antiques occupies the entire building. (Courtesy of Louis DeSantis.)

First published in 1858, the *Stafford Press* newspaper was run by James McLaughlin and his son Lewis. Robert G. Warner purchased the paper in 1935 and took it to new heights of fine writing and excellent local coverage. It was last published in 1976. Pictured around 1930 are, from left to right, Robert Sullivan, Dorothy Schofield, Harold Bruce Sr., Harold Bruce Jr., John Netto, Joseph Drobney, and George Grennan.

Originally the 1816 Parley Converse homestead, the Maple Grove Inn was opened in 1934 by Charles Guarco, who established an inn and restaurant, shown here. In 1973, the Maple Grove was bought by Pierre Courrieu, who opened Chez Pierre, a French restaurant that was a culinary landmark until it closed in 1999. The building was torn down to build a box store in 2015. (Courtesy of Louis DeSantis.)

John B. Piccin opened Piccin's Grocery and Fish Market on East Main Street in 1924. In 1948, John's son Aldo took over the business, transforming it into Deke's Confectionery Shop. Deke's was a favorite hangout for local teenagers for many years until its closing in 1962. Pictured are, from left to right, unidentified, John Piccin, Innocente Meneghin, unidentified, Bruno Piccin, Paul Constantini, and Lolo Piccin.

The Adams Block on East Main Street was built by Anthony Adams in 1907 to house his stove and plumbing business. The facade is galvanized iron embossed to look like granite. In 1927, the business was purchased by George W. Stevens Hardware. From 1963 until 1989, the business operated under the name Stevens Hardware and Plumbing, and was run by George's son Charles.

Built about 1845, this structure—today the Mill Pond Country Store—was primarily used as a general store. From 1882 to 1893, the building was used for a knitting works. Owned by Alpheus Weaver, this mill produced over 48,000 pairs of gloves and mittens in one year. In 2019, the business still feels like an old general store but with a deli counter, baked goods, and a dining area.

In 1905, George M. Barlow became the owner of the general store in West Stafford. George died in 1926 and his wife, Myrtle, ran the store until 1934, when she sold it to their son Milton. Milton went on to become a meteorologist and worked for the US Weather Bureau. He was also the weatherman for WTIC radio and Channel 3 television. Leonard's Auto Parts occupies the store in 2019.

Erose Belanger learned the cobbler trade from his father, Joseph, who opened a shoe repair shop in Stafford in 1919. Erose took over the Main Street business, operating it until 1971. He was also a part-time bondsman. If someone needed bail money, Erose would use his ladder to grab a shoebox containing cash from a top shelf. In 2019, Stafford Seamstress operates in this building.

The Great Atlantic & Pacific Tea Company, better known as the A&P, was the first chain grocery store in the country. In 1925, there were three Great Atlantic & Pacific Tea Company stores in the borough. In 1927, the three stores consolidated into one grocery next to the new town hall. In 1961, the store moved to a new building at the site of the old Springs House.

Around 1883, John M. Leach opened the Central Clothing House on Main Street, shown here. Active in town affairs, by 1915, Leach left the mercantile business to focus solely on being the borough warden. He also served for a time as a state representative. Wasserman's Department Store was later located here. It stood where the brick addition to Stafford House of Pizza is located in 2019.

In 1920, George Wood purchased a saloon on Main Street from James Sullivan and opened a meat market in the building, owning the business until his death in 1931. The building was then purchased by the Worker's Cooperative Union and torn down to build a new cooperative store. Shown from left to right are Thomas Young, Thomas Jensen, and George Wood.

Five

STAFFORD FAIR TO MOTOR SPEEDWAY

In 1870, the Stafford Fair was held for the first time by the newly formed Tolland County East Agricultural Society, later known as the Stafford Agricultural Society. The event was convened downtown, with the cattle show on the Springs House grounds, the exhibitions at Central Hall, and the horse racing on Main Street. The same year, the society bought land on West Street and built a racetrack and grandstand. The fair had exhibits of produce, handmade goods, and merchandise. Farmers competed for the largest squash and the best oxteam. The big racing events were the sulky races, but there were athletic competitions too. In 1918, no fair was held because of the worldwide influenza outbreak, and from 1936 to 1939 there was no fair because the society had gone bankrupt and the fairgrounds were sold off to pay debts.

In 1940, Clarence "Deke" Benton purchased the racetrack and grandstand and started up the fair again. The first day was Children's Day, when all students were let out of school early. The second day was Governor's Day, when the Connecticut governor would visit and give a speech. After World War II, auto racing became popular, and in 1948, Deke Benton sponsored auto races during the summer. Eventually, sulky racing was stopped and midget and stock car racing took its place. In 1959, Benton brought NASCAR to Stafford, putting Stafford on the map for short track racing.

In 1968, Deke Benton retired and the fair was bought by Malcolm Barlow, who built a new grandstand and black-topped the half-mile racetrack. The last Stafford Fair was held in 1969. In 1970, Jack Arute Sr. purchased the fairgrounds, and the Stafford Motor Speedway has been run by the Arute family since then.

The gateway to the Stafford Springs Agricultural Park, shown here in 1906, was west of the intersection of West and Park Streets. Starting in 1908, the trolley connecting Rockville to Stafford dropped off fairgoers at a trolley stop near this gate. Early on, most out-of-town fairgoers arrived in Stafford by train. The Central Vermont Railway even ran extra trains from Palmer, Massachusetts, on fair days.

Balloon Ascension at Fair Grounds, Stafford Springs Conn.

In 1882, the first hot-air balloon ascended over the Stafford Fair, becoming a crowd favorite. That year, Madame Carlotta landed in the treetops, though she subsequently had successful landings. However, accidents did happen—undoubtedly part of the crowd appeal. One year, the balloon went up in flames, and another time, strong winds collapsed the balloon in midair. No serious injuries were ever recorded.

This c. 1890 view looks across the racetrack to a full grandstand. The midway's location in the center of the track led to people being on the racetrack during races. Occasionally, a spectator was hit by a horse. Eventually, the midway was moved outside the racetrack, and an exhibition hall was built, which kept foot traffic off the track.

Parking problems at the 1899 fair involved horses and carriages, as shown here. Police tried their best to direct traffic to prevent accidents, but they still occurred. In 1900, after a day at the fair, an intoxicated carriage driver sped along Main Street, despite throngs of people and horses, sideswiping a parked surrey. The offending driver flipped his carriage over, but fortunately no serious injuries resulted.

This 1908 image of the dust clouds and flying hooves of harness racing appeared in the fair's 1909 Premier List and Program. At first held on Tuesdays through Thursdays, by 1944, the fair was held consistently Thursdays through Sundays. Admission for all three days in 1909 was $1.50 with a team and $1.00 without. It cost 50¢ to "admit" a car.

Events alternated between the racetrack and a stage viewable from the grandstand. Here are the starting moments of a footrace. Individuals and high school teams competed in running, walking, bicycling, and relay races. In 1879, John Sullivan won the five-mile race in 31 minutes. Stage acts, such as trained animals, acrobats, or vaudeville shows, entertained throughout the day.

Built in 1916, the exhibition hall, seen here, enabled the Agricultural Society to assemble all exhibits under one roof in a space four times as large as the old hall. At this time, various small structures were removed from the track's infield, creating an unobstructed view of the racetrack. In 2019, the hall still stands at the Stafford Motor Speedway.

A cornucopia of produce overflows the tables in the exhibition hall in 1922. A sign on the wall reads, "Gleanings of the field of L.E. Dimock." Standing between the tables is 78-year-old Luther Edwin Dimock, a West Stafford farmer who exhibited annually at Stafford and many other fairs in the state.

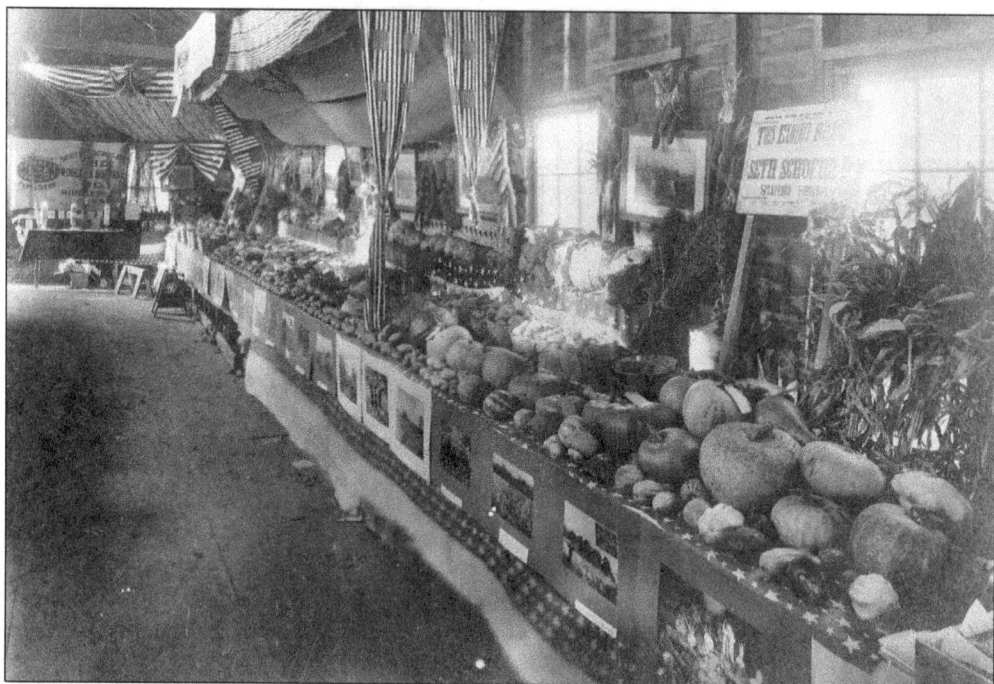

Agriculture remained important in Stafford in the 20th century. The produce in the foreground came from Seth Schofield's farm on Village Hill. In the late 1800s, a Stafford native, Ephraim H. Hyde, was pivotal in starting an agricultural school that taught farming and husbandry as a science. It evolved into the University of Connecticut. Hyde was also a founder of the Stafford Agricultural Society.

Farm animals galore were shown at the fair: horses, poultry, goats, and sheep. But the cattle parade, pictured, was keenly awaited. Ephraim H. Hyde was an innovative cattle breeder who worked toward improving the blood stock of cattle, particularly Devons, best suited for Stafford farms. By 1910, Stafford farmers began raising more cattle, and many small dairies were started.

In the fair's early years, trains of yoked oxen—all harnessed together—were driven to the fair. Here, about 20 pairs of oxen stand in front of the Pinney barn at the intersection of Upper and Leonard Roads in Stafford Hollow. These animals belonged to Benjamin Arnold and Edwin Pinney.

Until the early 1940s, the sulky races were the fair's biggest draw. Each year, the winner's purse increased, attracting sulky drivers from along the Eastern Seaboard to race at the Stafford Fair. Although gambling was discouraged and illegal, a bet could be placed downtown at the Springs House the night before a big race.

A sulky driver is awarded a silver platter for winning a race at the fair. Popularized in New England in the 1840s, harness racing involves a horse pulling a two-wheeled vehicle called a sulky. The driver sits between two bicycle-like wheels behind a U-shaped shaft connected by a harness to a well-trained horse. In 2019, the Serafin Sulky Company of Stafford Springs still makes wood sulkies in its small shop.

In 1908, Stafford High School seniors first sponsored a food booth at the fair. Proceeds funded the seniors' field trip to Washington, DC, the next spring. Pictured in 1940 are members of the class of 1941. Among those on the roof are Edward Panciera, Dorothy Piccin, Inez Innocenzi, and Mary Hanley, while Eleanor Driscoll tends the booth.

The Coleman Brothers of Middletown, Connecticut, are unloading their equipment in the 1940s. From 1919 until 1969, Coleman Brothers brought carnival rides, sideshows, and concession booths to the Stafford Fair. Beyond the trucks are, at left, the racetrack with grandstand and, at right, the exhibition hall. (Courtesy of Louis DeSantis.)

This 1942 photograph shows a small part of the midway. The fair this year was held despite restrictions on transportation because of World War II. The prizes were awarded in war bonds and stamps, and there could be no fireworks because of the need for blackouts at night.

This photograph shows the midway area on a busy day. Police worked to stop pickpockets, common in the early years of the fair. They also had an ongoing struggle with alcohol consumption and gambling. "Hard spirits" could generally be found by those looking, but were discouraged during the temperance movement and illegal during Prohibition. (Courtesy of Louis DeSantis.)

By the late 1940s, automobile thrill shows were part of the fair, complete with death-defying stunts such as loops and tailspins. Here, a car teeters on two wheels after leaving a ramp. In 1950, the highlighted act—Irish Horan and the Lucky Hell Drivers—shot a brand-new convertible out of a giant cannon. (Courtesy of Louis DeSantis.)

After World War II, interest in harness racing had waned, while auto racing was gaining ground. In May 1948, Clarence Benton began stock car racing on the track at the fairgrounds during the summer. By 1949, stock car racing became an event at the fair on the dirt track formerly used for harness racing. (Courtesy of Louis DeSantis.)

By 1949, regularly scheduled motorcycle racing began at the racetrack. There had been sporadic races as early as 1904. In 1953, the first race was run at night under electric lights. By 1959, motorcycle racing was included as an event, and harness racing had been discontinued. This photograph was taken by Shany Lorenzet.

In 1943, Clarence Benton built a roller-skating rink in the exhibition hall, which became a popular place for Christmas and Halloween parties. Polka nights and other types of dancing events were held here, too. Manager Jack Connors added lessons to the activities, and by 1950, the rink was open three nights a week. (Courtesy of Louis DeSantis.)

Before 1940, the Stafford Fairgrounds were active only during the fair and for some sports events. But Clarence Benton worked to make the complex bustle throughout the year. During World War II, he built a bowling alley on the ground floor of the exhibition hall, named Fairway Alleys. It offered league bowling and group bowling every night. (Courtesy of Louis DeSantis.)

Six

SOCIAL CLUBS, SPORTS, AND LEISURE

In the late 19th century, more people started having leisure time, previously only enjoyed by the wealthy. By the 1890s, the workweek for many mill workers had been reduced to five and a half days a week, and eight hours a day instead of 12. Social groups formed along religious, ethnic, economic, and other commonalities, most promoting fellowship, education, and charitable activities. Many social groups were active in Stafford, including the Stafford Grange, Knights of Columbus, Catholic Daughters of America, Little Theatre, Stafford Women's Club, and the Boys' Club. Ethnic groups in town included the German Club, Hibernian Society, and the Italian Benefit Society, known as the Italian Club, which is still active in 2019.

Sports were a favorite pastime in Stafford. After the Civil War, the love of baseball spread across the country. For a time, almost every ethnic group, neighborhood, factory, and major business in town sponsored a team. For several years, Stafford had enough teams for a town-wide league, and fans could watch baseball nearly every day of the week. Women's softball became popular around 1940. The velocipede was introduced to Stafford in 1869 and a velocipede "school" was opened in Oronoco Hall on Main Street. In 1898, the Stafford Country Club was formed, and a golf course was built on lower Monson Road opposite the Stafford Springs Cemetery. The Stafford Boys' Club was formed in 1910 and had a gym and bowling alley in a building at the corner of Willington and Westford Avenues. Basketball, hockey, football, and bowling were popular, too.

Entertainment such as circuses, fairs, musical groups, vaudeville shows, plays, and readings became common. Stage performances were often given at Oronoco Hall, the Comique Theatre, Warren Memorial Town Hall on Main Street, and Memorial Hall in Stafford Hollow. Around the time of World War I, movies began to be shown in all these locations. Parades were a favorite way to celebrate Independence Day and, later, Memorial and Labor Days. There was no shortage of interesting events in Stafford in the late 1800s and early 1900s.

This 1870s stereopticon shows a circus tent on Willington Avenue, north of the current site of the Stafford Fire Department. In the foreground is the Willimantic River. The large white building at upper left, at the intersection of Willington and Westford Avenues, was the Stafford Boys' Club, now an apartment building. Partially visible above the tent is the Dennis Grain Mill.

The Stafford Country Club was a private golf club founded in 1898 by local golf enthusiasts. They constructed a clubhouse and six-hole golf course, soon expanded to nine holes. In 1915, they merged with the Stafford Golf Company. A new clubhouse was built in 1919 (pictured). In 1942, the property was purchased by Strazza Post, American Legion, and remodeled for use as a Legion home.

Stafford caught the "baseball fever" that gripped the entire nation from the late 19th century until well into the 20th century. Most towns sponsored a team to compete against nearby towns. Great civic pride was displayed in support of the local team, posing here around 1910 in Hyde Park, the site of home games.

In 1907, Stafford won the championship of the Bi-State Base-Ball League and was awarded a silver cup given by the *Springfield Union* newspaper. This semipro league was comprised of teams from Indian Orchard, Ludlow, Monson, Springfield, Stafford, and Ware. They played a 20-game schedule. Stafford's home field was at the fairgrounds, site of today's Stafford Motor Speedway.

Pictured around 1942 is Stafford Worsted's women's softball team. From left to right are (first row) Roland Simpson, Lena Kurek, Lena Bagley, Louise Scussel, Stella Marconi, and Harold Boyer; (second row) Esther Panciera, Anita Julian, Mary DaNadai, Dorothy Baldracchi, and Mildred Tonidandel; (third row) Marguerite Panciera, Irene McQuaid, Italia Panciera, Margaret Davis, and Constance Corsini.

The Stafford Olympics football team finished their season with only one defeat on their record in 1933. Having defeated the All Rockville team in two out of three playoff games, they claimed the title of Tolland County champions. Started in 1926, the Olympics played for over 40 years. Home games were at Keefe Plain, now called Olympic Field.

Members of McCormick Drug Store's bowling team, shown in 1959, were champions of the Girls Glamour Bowling League. The league bowled at the Bradley Bowling Alleys on the second floor of the Oronoco Block on Main Street. From left to right are Helen Dombeck, Marilyn Bachiochi, Carrie Curnan, Esther DaRos, Theresa Innocenzi, and Celia Curnan.

The Stafford Olympics basketball team was active from 1922 to 1957. The semipro team played games against other such teams from throughout southern New England. Shown is the 1930–1931 squad. From left to right are Albert Ricci, Robert MacLagan, Harold Smith, Rudolph Fickinger, Edward Ware, Francis Ward, Charles Ward, Edward Bidorini, Roy Panciera, Edwin Schubler, and Raymond Houle (kneeling).

The Stafford Kacey Juniors basketball team was sponsored by the Felix J. O'Neill Knights of Columbus Council 1395 of St. Edward Parish. Members of the 1946–1947 team are, from left to right, (first row) Alexander Paolini, Leo Sfreddo, Bernard Niderno, Norman Palardy, and Glenn Tonoli; (second row) Mariano Calchera, Roy Cooley, unidentified, William Kology, Theodore Cockburn, and coach Raymond Houle.

Local amateur hockey started in 1947 with a team sponsored by the American Legion Strazza-Tonoli Post 26, which competed regionally and played home games on a rink near the American Legion on Monson Road. The 1950–1951 team shown here belonged to the Connecticut Valley Hockey League and competed against Manchester, Somersville, Agawam, Indian Orchard, Holyoke, Chicopee, and Springfield. All league games were at the Springfield Coliseum in West Springfield.

Stafford police chief Bill Silk often took local boys to Boston Red Sox games at Fenway Park. Ready for a trip around 1938 are, from left to right, (first row) Joseph "Shat" Corsini; (second row) John Keirans, Louis Mattesen, Norman Palardy, Stephen Kaminski, Louis Mattarelli, Gordon Goodell, and Maurice Fitzgerald; (third row) William Emhoff, Andrew Mattesen, Frank Jakobsen, Carl Mattesen, and Chief Silk.

Charles R. Newton of Stafford Springs was a champion bicycle racer during the 1890s, the golden age of the sport. He raced as an amateur for four years and then turned professional for three more years. He rode the so-called Grand Circuit throughout the East and Midwest, setting many records and winning numerous awards. Newton became a textile designer and later was superintendent at Smith & Cooley.

The Grange was organized in January 1874 as a fraternal organization promoting the social and economic needs of farmers. Stafford's Grange was the first one chartered in Connecticut. The building, shown here in the 1920s, is owned by Stafford Grange No. 1, which meets on the second floor. On the first floor is the Stafford Post Office in Stafford Hollow.

The Citizens Band, organized about 1880, is the earliest known band in Stafford. Its music was in popular demand at local celebrations, commemorations, parades, and civic events. The musicians also entertained for "shore dinners" at the Crystal Lake Grove on Crystal Lake in Ellington. Their last known performance was in July 1918.

The Phoenix Liberty Band was founded in 1918 by employees of the Phoenix Woolen Company in Hydeville. Among the musicians shown are Ernest Clemens Schmidt, Fred Lynch, Carl Woods, William Dunham, Arthur Smith, Paul Schmidt, Frederick Smith, William Lasbury, and Hugh Jenkins.

The Italian Band was organized in 1915 under the direction of Prof. Berado Sbraccia, a noted composer, conductor, and clarinetist. After months of practice, the band made its initial public appearance on Sunday evening, July 18, 1915, with a well-received concert in Hyde Park. For many years, the group presented an annual series of concerts, also participating in local and regional community parades and events.

In 1919, Stafford had two reasons to celebrate: the 200th anniversary of its founding in 1719 and the end of World War I the previous November. The world was at peace, and Stafford's veterans had returned home. In October, a three-day celebration began with a lavish parade. This peace float was sponsored by the Rhode Island Worsted Company.

The parade on October 15, 1919, included this float sponsored by the Odd Fellows and its female auxiliary, the Myriad Rebekah Lodge. The women on the float are, from left to right, Margaret Vollans, Gladys Cummings, and unidentified. The driver is Embert Curtis. In the background is the First National Bank building on East Main Street.

Seven

EDUCATION AND FAITH

The history of religion in Stafford begins with Congregationalism, which was the "church of the standing order." In 1721, the first church was built on Stafford Street, and all residents were required to attend and pay tax to support this Congregational church. In 1761, West Stafford was granted the right to have its own church, and the town was split into East and West Parishes. The first West Stafford Congregational Church was built on Hampden Hill in 1764. About this time, other Protestant teachings were introduced in the region. The first Universalist church in the state was built in West Stafford before 1800. Methodist and Baptist services were being held in the area, and fewer people were attending the Congregational churches. The population of Stafford was growing exponentially as immigrants moved into town to work in the mills. Other denominations such as Episcopal, Roman Catholic, Lutheran, and Spiritualist joined the assortment of churches in town. Between 1833 and 1878, fifteen churches were built in Stafford's growing villages.

Education was almost as important to the settlers as religion. The first school was built on Stafford Street before 1800. In 1761, when the town was split into two parishes, each parish was broken into school districts, 17 in total. Each was self-governed and was required to build and maintain a schoolhouse. Ten of the one-room schools built between 1799 and 1884 are still standing in 2019, and all but one are private homes.

In 1856, control of the schools was given to the town, and education took a positive new direction, resulting in the consolidation of districts. The first Stafford High School was built in the borough in 1883, and elementary schools were built in the larger districts. In 1950, the last village schoolhouse was closed. Today, there is a campus of schools on Levinthal Run providing an education for Stafford students in grades 2 through 12—Stafford Elementary School, Stafford Middle School, and Stafford High School. The old West Stafford and Staffordville schools are used for pre-kindergarten through first-grade classes.

The Stafford Springs Congregational Church was an imposing structure built on Haymarket Square in 1850. Visible from all directions when entering town, the church was destroyed in the flood of 1877. A wall of water hit the building, and the spire crashed to the ground. Two men had taken refuge on the steps but were washed away with the church, the flood's only casualties.

Post-flood, the Stafford Springs congregation quickly rebuilt at the same site, dedicating a new Congregational church in 1878. Members eschewed the traditional white Greek Revival design, opting instead for the modest Gothic Revival style. The stringcourse (stone blocks running above the foundation) and the steps had been part of the old Stafford Street church, which was being dismantled at that time.

The interior of the Stafford Springs Congregational Church, with the original stenciling, is shown in this undated image. The interior was remodeled in 1954 when a new chancel was built, and the floor was carpeted. In 1969, a truck driving down East Main Street lost its brakes and crashed through the front wall of the church into the nave.

The original Methodist church in Stafford Springs was built in 1833 at the corner of Green and West Main Streets. Later, a new church was built closer to the village center in 1866. The old building was sold in 1874 and moved to Mashapaug Lake in Union, as seen in this c. 1895 photograph.

In 1866, requiring larger quarters and a more central location, a new Methodist church was built in Stafford Springs on land donated by Julius and Orrin Converse. The original 135-foot-tall steeple was damaged during a storm in 1917 and rebuilt at a reduced height. In 1958, due to severe deterioration, the tall steeple was replaced by a shorter tapered spire.

In 1880, the Methodist church celebrated the 50th anniversary of the Methodist church being in Stafford Springs. The altar shown here in 1880 is decorated for the celebration. A new pipe organ was installed in memory of Solva and Parley Converse. A church membership of 140 in 1865 grew to 271 by 1878.

The first Roman Catholics to settle in Stafford were Irish laborers who came to town before 1850 to work on the railroad. By 1866, construction of St. Edward Church began, using granite donated by Cornelius Flaherty from his local quarry. Work was completed in 1868. Rev. Peter Shahan was the first resident pastor of St. Edward Church.

In 1887, St. Edward Church was greatly enlarged to accommodate 600 parishioners—200 more than the old church. Renovations included an expanded sanctuary and the addition of transepts and two side towers. Around 1890, the rectory, which is still in use in 2019, was constructed next to the church.

BEHOLD THY KING COMETH

In 1872, an Episcopalian group began meeting in Stafford in a rented room called Mission Hall, shown above at Christmas in 1875. The hall was located in the Chamberlin Block on Main Street. Plans to build a church were impeded by the Panic of 1873 and the flood of 1877. However, with help from the diocese, a lot on Spring Street was bought and a church erected. The first service was held there in December 1877. Grace Episcopal Church, shown at left around 1880, stood alone before Julius Converse built his office, which later became the public library. The mineral springs well is visible alongside the church.

In 1914, about 80 families started gathering in Willington to hold Lutheran services in their native Slovak language. In 1922, they converted the Teutonia Clubhouse, a German social club on West Main Street, into a church. Many of these Czech and Slovak families had immigrated to Pennsylvania and later relocated to Stafford. In 1967, the name was changed to the Holy Trinity Lutheran Church.

The Baptist community in Stafford officially began in 1809, and for years shared a meetinghouse on Stafford Street with the Universalist church. In 1834, the congregation built its own church, shown here, in Stafford Hollow on Leonard Road, an area known for generations as Baptist Hill. The oldest standing church in town, it has a Paul Revere bell.

Starting in 1814, the Universalist and Baptist congregations shared a joint meetinghouse on Stafford Street. However, in 1845, the Universalists built their own church in Stafford Hollow, shown above around 1895. It is believed that the iron railings on the portico of the church are from the foundry in Stafford Hollow. An early minister was Rev. Daniel P. Livermore, who served from 1846 to 1851. His wife, Mary R. Livermore, became a nationally respected advocate of women's suffrage and temperance. She returned to Stafford Hollow many times to give well-attended lectures at the Spiritualist Hall. Built in 1904, the Universalist parsonage, shown below about 1910, was located across from the Baptist church. It boasted a large assembly room for youth gatherings, and was later leased to the town for a kindergarten. The house was demolished in 2008.

In 1859, former members of the Stafford Street Congregational Church built the Congregational church in Staffordville seen here. Ninety years later, this church captured the national spotlight after choosing Rev. Roland T. Heacock as its pastor, an African American Yale-educated minister. He was quoted in *Look* magazine as saying that he was "chosen for his Christianity, not his color." Reverend Heacock served the church for nine years.

To meet the spiritual needs of Roman Catholics in the Staffordville area, St. Joseph Chapel, seen around 1895—was built in 1878 at a cost of $500. Originally seating 60, the building was enlarged in 1881 and 1900 as the congregation grew. A 1954 expansion extended the sanctuary and increased the seating again. In 2016, the building was sold to the Staffordville Congregational Church.

Built in 1860, the Methodist church in Staffordville stood on the north side of East Street, just beyond Colburn Road. Services were held until 1947, when the congregation disbanded. A few concerned residents purchased the building, renaming it the Staffordville Community Center. Used for local meetings and social events, the building was demolished in 1981 despite efforts to save it.

West Stafford residents formed the West Parish in 1764 and built their own church. In 1839, a new edifice was erected atop Hampden Hill. In 1854, the church was moved to the new center of the village at the bottom of the hill. In 2019, the Second Congregational Church of Stafford still stands at the intersection of West Stafford and Crystal Lake Roads.

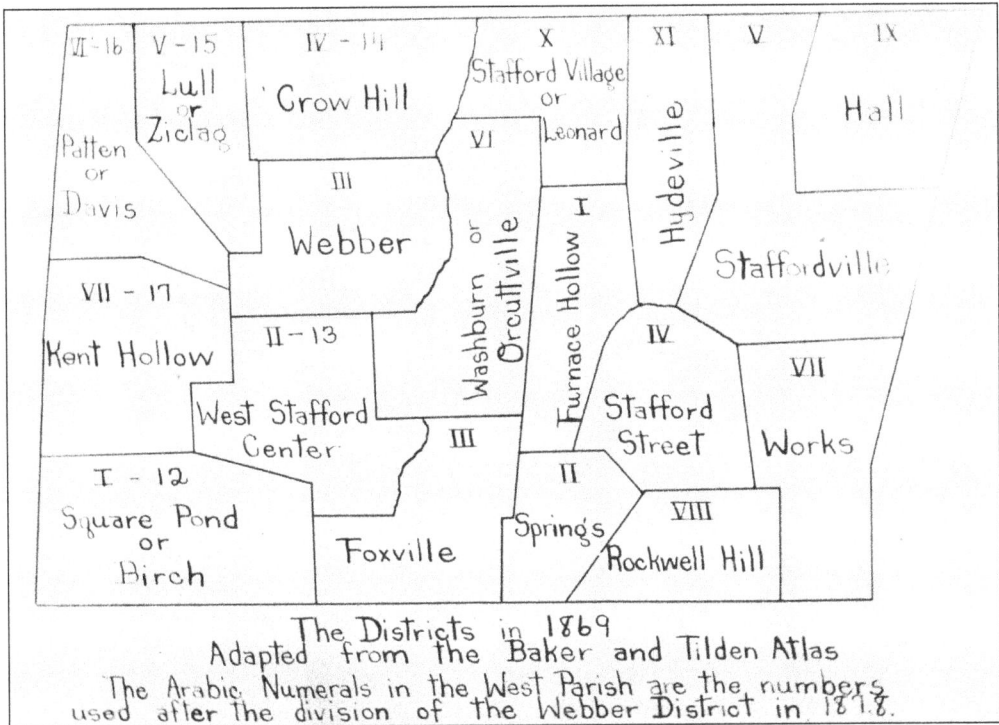

The Districts in 1869
Adapted from the Baker and Tilden Atlas
The Arabic Numerals in the West Parish are the numbers
used after the division of the Webber District in 1818.

This hand-drawn map of unknown origin was published in Earl M. Witt's *History of the Schools of Stafford* (1946). It shows recognized Stafford school districts between 1761 and 1899. Each district built its own one-room schoolhouse and had its own calendar and curriculum. In 1856, the town took over control of the schools, although the districts remained in place until consolidation in 1899.

Built on Stafford Street about 1780, the first schoolhouse had a gambrel roof and a steeple with a bell. That building was replaced in 1883 by the schoolhouse shown here around 1910. Most one-room schoolhouses in town were similar. In the photograph, only Ruth Larned (first row, second from left) and Chester Goodell (first row, third from left) have been identified. (Courtesy of Esther DaRos.)

The Patten District Schoolhouse, in Stafford's northwest corner, was used until the 1930s, after which it was converted into a home. In 2005, the building was donated to the Stafford Historical Society with the stipulation that it be moved from its site. Historical society members and town residents banded together to dismantle the building, move the pieces, and reconstruct the school at Heritage Park in Stafford, at the intersection of Stafford Street and Route 190.

Built as a one-room schoolhouse in 1869, the West Stafford Schoolhouse was expanded to two rooms in 1895. Until 1941, this school had no indoor plumbing. Retired in 1950 when a modern West Stafford Elementary School was built nearby, this was the town's last small schoolhouse. Since the 1950s, it has been a private home.

The first Stafford High School on High Street, built in 1883 and shown here in the 1930s, was enlarged twice to accommodate grades seven and eight. By the 1930s, a new school was needed. Although the Great Depression made funding difficult, the town secured a Public Works Administration grant that helped finance building a new school, which opened in 1939. The grant stipulated demolition of the "Old Red School."

In 1874, St. Edward's opened a one-story school with 75 students, which helped ease some crowding in downtown schools. It was replaced in 1886 by a two-story structure, shown here in the 1950s, with classrooms on the first floor and an assembly hall on the second floor. It remained in use until 1954, when St. Edward's built a modern school. St. Edward's School closed its doors in 2016.

This commodious school in Staffordville originated in 1848 as a two-room, two-story building. From 1878 to 1882, the number of students had increased by 100 in this village alone. By 1883, the schoolhouse was doubled in size and moved back from the road. In 1929, the current Staffordville School was built, and this school was decommissioned and became a residence.

Pinney School was built in 1895 to consolidate the Stafford Hollow and Hydeville school districts. The land was donated by Edwin C. Pinney, a prominent Stafford businessman, and his wife, Esther. A four-room school intended to accommodate 35 to 40 pupils in each class, it had two furnaces but no indoor plumbing. The Pinney School was used as a school until 1982 and as board of education offices from 1985 to 2006.

In 1922, a new elementary school was built behind the first Stafford High School. In this image, the high school is at left and the new school is at right. Known as the Borough Elementary School, it was used as a school for 85 years. In 2007, this school was decommissioned because the new Stafford Elementary School had opened. In 2019, the building stands unused.

The old Staffordville schoolhouse had grown outdated and overcrowded by 1928 and needed repair. In 1929, a new Staffordville School was built on the shores of Staffordville Lake. It served as one of three town elementary schools after the one-room schoolhouses were discontinued. Since 2007, when a new elementary school was built on Levinthal Run, the Staffordville School has been used for pre-kindergarten through first-grade students.

In January 1939, Stafford High School students started attending the new school built on land in Hyde Park where the Woodlawn mansion once stood. A site near the fairgrounds was also considered, but the Hyde Park site was selected. The building, shown here around 1939, was later used as a middle and intermediate school, renamed in honor of longtime superintendent of schools Earl M. Witt. It closed in 2007.

Following World War II, school enrollments increased dramatically as more students finished high school and went on to college. Stafford's school population soon outgrew its high school building. In January 1968, after seven years of double sessions for grades 7–12 at the school in Hyde Park, Stafford opened a new, 36-classroom high school on Orcuttville Road. In 2019, after several expansions, this building is still in use.

Eight

THOSE WHO PROTECT AND SERVE

Stafford has been represented in almost every war and conflict that the United States has experienced. Sixty-five men from town responded to the "Lexington Alarm" and marched off to fight for independence during the American Revolution. During the Civil War, over 300 men from Stafford joined the fight, and almost half of them died during the war from injury or disease. In the First World War, 209 men and one woman served in the armed services. In World War II, over 760 men and women from town enlisted over the four years that the country was at war. Since then, more than 200 Stafford residents have served in various conflicts.

The first fire department in town was organized in 1872. Fire was the nemesis of woolen textile mills because one spark could start an inferno. Both the minute particles of wool fibers in the air and oil from wool were highly flammable. Eventually, fire departments were started in Staffordville and West Stafford to help reduce the response time to outlying areas. Today, Stafford has two fire departments that work together responding to the town's emergencies.

In 1883, the borough had two to three police officers, and their duties included lighting the streetlamps on Main Street at dusk. For several years, more controversy arose from the streetlights not being lit than about any type of crime. The temperance movement in the late 19th century and the Volstead Act in 1920, making Prohibition the law, increased the need for both local and state police officers. In 1922, the Connecticut State Police established a barracks in Stafford Springs to help fight illegal manufacturing and sales of alcohol. Eventually, the state police department was augmented with a resident state trooper and local police, whose office is located in the former train station.

Col. Charles Warren, Stafford businessman and Civil War veteran, left money in his will to build a monument in memory of Civil War veterans. In 1924, the Soldiers' Monument was dedicated in Hyde Park. The monument was designed by R.L. McGovern of Hartford, and the sculptures were done by Frederic Wellington Ruckstull, a renowned New York City sculptor. Warren also left money to build the Warren Memorial Town Hall.

In 1897, the local chapter of the Grand Army of the Republic, an organization of Civil War veterans, dedicated a monument in memory of the Stafford men who served in the Civil War. Located in the Stafford Springs Cemetery, the memorial of granite supports a Rodman gun that was cast in 1850. The monument was made by the Stafford Springs Monumental Works, owned by Arthur W. Kingsbury.

A c. 1916 Memorial Day parade heads up Main Street toward the Stafford Springs Cemetery. Walking in front of the marching band is a Civil War veteran and member of the Grand Army of the Republic. The men in lines behind the band are Civil War veterans and sons of veterans. Note the Comique Theater, which is now the Palace, a music venue.

For the Memorial Day celebration on May 30, 1919, all Stafford veterans of the Great War—the only world war, at that point—gathered for a photograph. This was the first time all World War I veterans of Stafford had come together since the war ended on November 11, 1918. The men are posing at the side entrance of the Stafford Springs House.

During World War II, Civil Defense volunteers fulfilled many duties on the home front. Members of the Ground Observer Corps were trained to spot and identify enemy aircraft to protect the United States from an air attack. Armed with a pair of binoculars, airplane identification books, and flash cards, they manned airplane spotting towers such as this one located off Leonard Road.

Many pieces of history were sacrificed for the war effort, such as this steam-powered, hand-pulled water pump from the Stafford Springs Fire Department. Due to shortages of all types of metal during World War II, municipalities and organizations ran campaigns for scrap collection. The goal of Stafford's 1943 scrap metal campaign was 305 tons. The Scrap for Victory campaigns allowed the United States to build airplanes, tanks, and warships.

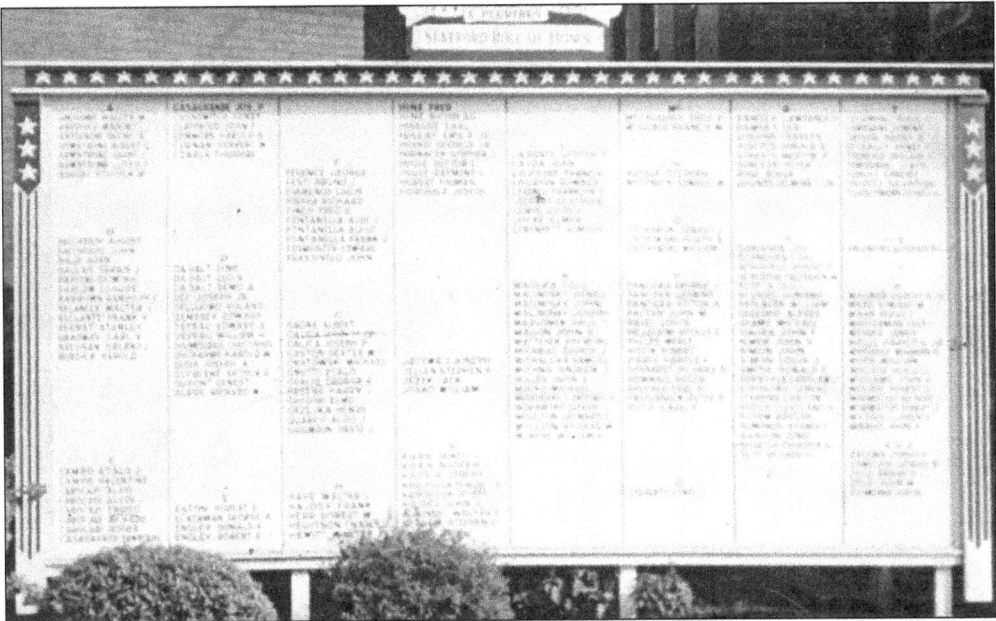

In 1942, Stafford erected a Wall of Honor in front of the town hall listing all the men and women from Stafford who were in the military. By September 1943, the wooden wall was rebuilt to display all the names of the servicemen and servicewomen. By the end of the war, over 760 Stafford residents had served in the armed forces.

Today, Stafford has a Wall of Honor for 20th-century veterans in the Stafford Veterans Memorial Park at Olympic Circle, not far from the American Legion Post 26. This wall lists all Stafford residents who served in World War I, World War II, the Korean War, the Vietnam War, Lebanon and Beirut, Desert Storm, and special operations. This ongoing project will add Stafford veterans' names from the 21st century in Phase IV.

The theme of this Fourth of July parade in 1940 was the "Spirit of '76." After the Fife and Drum Corps is the American Legion Color Guard. Harold W. Bruce is walking at right. In the background is the lower end of East Main Street: the Stafford Hotel, at the left, with a balcony of onlookers; Piccin's Market and Soda Fountain (center); and George Stevens' Hardware Store (at right).

The first Stafford Springs Fire Department, Torrent Fire Engine Company No. 1, incorporated in 1872 with 32 men, a hand pumper, and hand-drawn hose carriage. The same year, the department assembled in Haymarket Square in front of the old Congregational church, where the stone church stands today. In 1884, this fire department became part of the Borough of Stafford Springs. (Courtesy of Louis DeSantis.)

110

In 1872, a firehouse was built next to the Stafford Springs House, but this building and all the equipment were washed away in the flood of 1877. In 1878, a new firehouse was built on the same spot and new equipment was obtained. In 1920, the department purchased an American LaFrance motorized fire engine, shown here, for $11,500. In 2019, the former firehouse is the home of Shamrock Cleaners.

This is the Stafford Springs Fire Department in January 1954. From left to right are (first row) Joseph Young, Robert Rounds, Edmund Mattarelli, Fire Chief Wilfred Sabourin, Louis Mattarelli, Dino Oldrini, and Theodore Baxter; (second row) Fred Bolieau, Robert Beaulieu, Fire Marshal Edward Gilman, Foreman Aldo Armelin, James Greene, Norman Gagne, Walter Hare, William Angley, Leonard Bouderau, Chief Engineer Walter Schumann, and Assistant Chief Woodrow Pitkat; (third row) Romeo Panciera.

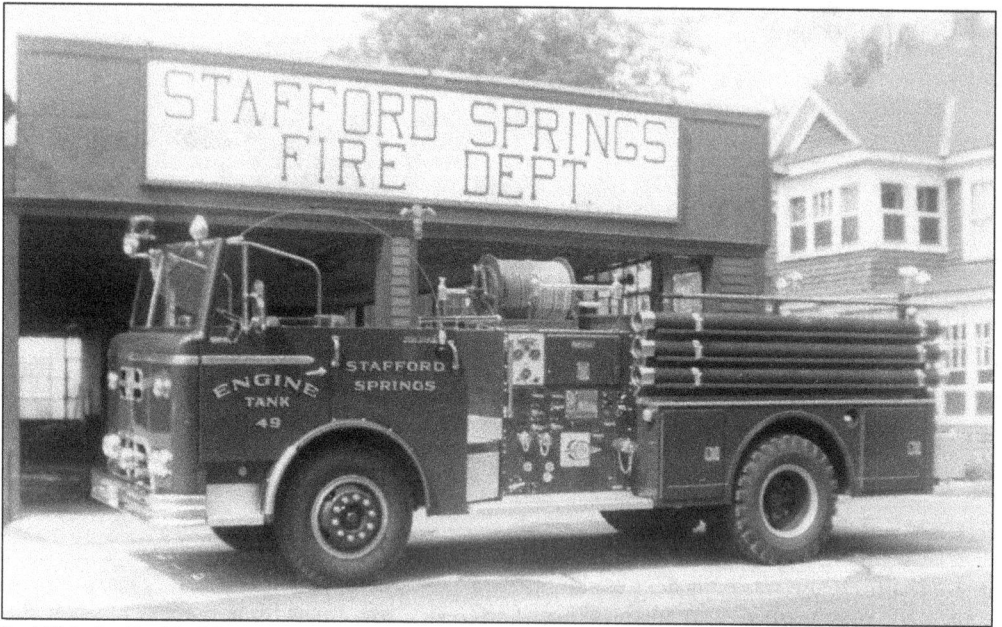

In 1956, the Stafford Springs Fire Department was relocated to West Main Street in a building that had previously housed the Central Garage. The department remained here until 1994, when a new firehouse was built on Willington Avenue. The Stafford Springs Fire Department was disbanded in 1999 due to unresolved management issues with the town. (Courtesy of Louis DeSantis.)

A volunteer fire department was formed in Staffordville in 1934 with 24 charter members. In 1936, the Stafford Fire Department No. 1 was incorporated. The first firehouse was an unused dance hall and garage on the property of Schwanda and Sons' Button Company. A fire alarm bell was fashioned from a locomotive wheel rim and hung near the Staffordville Post Office, along with a sledgehammer for striking it.

For its first three years, the Staffordville Fire Department responded to fires with a Nash touring car that had been converted into a fire truck, painted bright red, and equipped with a chemical tank, four fire extinguishers, and two ladders. In 1937, the department was able to purchase its first truck. In 1951, a new two-story firehouse was completed on Colburn Road, near the old one.

The West Stafford Fire Department was formed in 1946, and the following year, the new two-story firehouse on West Stafford Road was completed. The department used borrowed fire equipment until it was able to purchase its first truck in March 1949. This truck was the first in town to carry 1,000 gallons of water. In 1995, a new firehouse was built across from the West Stafford School. (Courtesy of the West Stafford Fire Department.)

One of the longest-serving police officers in Stafford Springs was Louis Helm. First appointed as a borough police officer in 1885, he went on to become deputy sheriff and, later, chief of police. In 1937, Helm was still working when he suffered a stroke at the age of 84. He was said to be one of the oldest active law enforcement officers in the country at that time.

Around 1950, the members of the Stafford Springs Police Department pose on the steps of Warren Memorial Town Hall. From left to right are (first row) Joseph Young, Herman Schmidt, George Benzel, and Thomas Young; (second row) Police Commissioner Elric Ramsey, Florina Zelz, Chief William Silk, William Duval, and Borough Warden Aldo Peloni; (third row) Robert Beaulieu, Lester Russell, and Woodrow Pitkat.

In 1922, the Connecticut State Police chose Stafford Springs as a strategic location for a state police barracks because of the town's location on the principal driving route between Hartford and Boston. The police rented rooms from Mattesen Service Station on Willington Avenue for five years. Officers are shown here in 1926 with state vehicles. (Courtesy of Louis DeSantis.)

In 1927, a new state police barracks was built on Buckley Highway in Stafford Springs. The two-story building had a fieldstone facade on the first floor and shingles on the second floor. In 1937, after expansion, shown here, it provided housing for the police and jail cells. In 1995, the barracks moved to Tolland. Today, Stafford owns the building, which houses the Stafford Community Center. (Courtesy of Louis DeSantis.)

In 1912, the first hospital in Tolland County opened for patients in Stafford Springs. Cyril and Julia Johnson, owners of Johnson Woolen Mill, gifted $275,000 to build and maintain the new hospital. The facility had 30 beds, one operating room, one maternity room, central heating, electric lighting, and inside plumbing, just to name a few amenities. By 1975, the hospital had expanded to 65 beds.

In 1975, a modern four-story, 78-bed facility opened in West Stafford on Route 190. The new Johnson Memorial Hospital had two high-voltage x-ray machines, a high-tech ventilation system, and its own water system, sewage system, and emergency power. Today, Johnson Memorial is a 92-bed facility. The old hospital, which stood empty for eight years, was sold and turned into Memorial Apartments. (Courtesy of Louis DeSantis.)

Nine

DISASTERS

Stafford has had its share of fires and blizzards, but the three most destructive disasters were floods that occurred in 1877, 1938, and 1955. Stafford's industrial growth along the rivers made the town susceptible to damaging flooding. The March 1877 deluge involved land bordering Furnace Brook, running from Staffordville Lake to its convergence with Middle River in Stafford Springs, where the worst of the inundation occurred. The dam at Staffordville burst, sending a torrent of water rushing south through Hydeville and Stafford Hollow toward Stafford Springs. Although there was serious damage done along the way, the worst was in Stafford Springs, with its high concentration of structures. A wall of water 20 feet high hit Haymarket Square, and within two minutes wiped out almost every building in its path.

The floods of 1938 and 1955 were both caused by hurricanes. The Great Hurricane of 1938 is said to have been the most powerful storm to hit the Northeast in the 20th century. The US Weather Bureau failed to predict the potential of the storm and did not have accurate readings of where it would hit land. Therefore, no one was prepared for what was about to ensue. Coastal communities in the Northeast were particularly hard hit, and over 680 people were killed. There were no fatalities in Stafford.

In 1955, two back-to-back hurricanes, Carol and Diane, dropped over 20 inches of rain in Connecticut. The wind damage was not like in 1938, but the flooding was just as bad. In 1938, Rhode Island had been hit hardest, but in 1955, it was Connecticut that suffered the most damage, particularly in mill towns. In Stafford, 17 businesses and five mills experienced extensive damage. This flood led to the eventual completion of a town-wide watershed project to prevent this type of flooding from occurring again.

On March 25, 1877, the dam on Staffordville Lake gave way due to excessive rain that raised the water level beyond the dam's capacity. The deluge traveled south along Furnace Brook from Staffordville to Stafford Springs, destroying nine dams. On horseback, 39-year-old Edwin C. Pinney rode ahead of the floodwaters to warn inhabitants of the valley. The Congregational church, three tenement houses, the bank, and the Crane store were just a few of the buildings destroyed by the flood. A stereopticon, above, shows the Granite Mill on the right, part of American Woolen Company today, and beyond it the void where the Congregational church had stood. The Springs House is in the distance. Below is the area in front of the Springs House with railroad cars filled with coal and wool scattered about.

The view above, in 1877, shows the devastation in the area between the railroad station and Willington Avenue. The three-story building in the distance still stands at the corner of Westford and Willington Avenues; it was the Boys' Club for many years. The building to its right with the tall chimney was the E.C. Dennis Grain Mill. All the buildings in the low-lying area were destroyed. The stereopticon below shows the washed out railroad bed and a few buildings of C.J. Holmes Coal and Lumber. This is where the Stafford Fire Department is today. Willington Avenue is visible going up the hill. In all, the water took about 57 minutes to reach downtown from Staffordville, and the destruction downtown took a total of two minutes.

The Great New England Hurricane of 1938 struck Connecticut unexpectedly on September 21. Potentially heavy rain had been forecast, but when the wind topped 100 miles per hour, residents realized this was not a normal storm. The strong wind snapped pine trees—hundreds in Hyde Park alone—and uprooted hardwood trees, sending some flying through the air. Above, in a view looking west down East Main Street, is the scene after the trees had been cleared from the road. The photograph below faces east at the corner of West Main and High Streets toward St. Edward Church. The building on the left was the Southern New England Telephone office from 1930 to 1953 These two buildings were later demolished; today, this is the site of the CVS parking lot.

The 1938 hurricane dropped over six inches of rain into already swollen rivers that had been rising due to a rainstorm several days before. The rain and flooding occurred first, and then the winds began. Flooding was so bad that the town was almost inaccessible. In 1955, two back-to-back hurricanes within eight days, Carol and Diane, dropped over 20 inches of rain in Connecticut. Flooded tributaries inundated Stafford's two major waterways, Furnace Brook and Middle River, particularly near their point of convergence in Stafford Springs. The railroad station had water halfway up the walls. The basement of the library was completely flooded, and the first floor was covered with 12 inches of water. A flooded Haymarket Square in 1938, above, and 1955, below, are almost indistinguishable from each other.

The 1955 flood caused major damage to roads and bridges, just as the 1938 flood had done. Seen above is the back end of a school bus that had been washed downstream and wedged under the bridge crossing Middle River at River Road. The combination of the flood and the bus resulted in this bridge being declared one of 33 in the state that were impassable. The bridge in Orcuttville was also on this list, because its roadbed had been washed out. Damage to roads and bridges was surveyed throughout the state using helicopters. Below, a helicopter was sent to Stafford to assess relief needs. The helicopter grazed a pine tree top as it started to land at the Borough School, and it crashed into the Mullins house on Howland Avenue. One marine was injured.

In March 1888, New England suffered the worst blizzard on record. Snow fell from Sunday evening to Wednesday morning. A fierce wind persisted in blowing the snow into drifts reaching 15 feet in some places. Although more than 400 people died in the Northeast due to the storm, no one in Stafford succumbed. In Staffordville, Dexter Colburn and family could not exit their house because it was surrounded with 58 inches of snow. The following week, rain fell and there was worry that the streams would start flooding, but the cold persisted long enough for the snow to melt gradually without causing another disaster. These two views of Main Street show the aftermath of the blizzard.

On May 26, 1917, a fire began in a haystack in Gary's Livery barn, which stood behind the G.H. Baker Block. The fire spread through the barn's walls and leapt across a narrow driveway to Baker's, which had been built in 1878. Despite the best efforts of the Torrent Fire Department, both the livery and Baker's were completely destroyed. This is the current site of Warren Memorial Town Hall.

In January 1904, a fire broke out in a storefront on lower Main Street. The temperature, which was about zero, made fighting the fire extremely difficult because the water was freezing on the exterior of the building while the fire was still raging within. The facade, resembling an ice palace, was a popular attraction until it melted almost two weeks later.

In 1929, Woodlawn mansion in Hyde Park was badly damaged by fire. The blaze occurred within 12 hours of the building being sold for scrap. In 1911, the town had purchased Julius Converse's estate, including the house, to establish a public park as outlined in the bequest of Isaac Perkins Hyde. Despite talk of converting the mansion into a high school, the building remained vacant.

In April 1959, the Springs House burned. The hotel stood for over 150 years. Many rooms had been converted into apartments, and a physician had set up his practice on the first floor. The building was badly damaged, and the owner, a Manchester investment firm, opted to tear it down. Faulty wiring was found to be the cause of the fire.

BIBLIOGRAPHY

Armelin, Allen A. *Torrent Fire Engine Co. No. 1*. Stafford Springs, CT: Stafford Press, 1975.
Dutton, Bruce G. *From Hosses to Autos: Harry Bradley*. Self-published, 2007.
———. *Orcuttville*. Self-published, 2011.
———. *Stafford in the Civil War*. Self-published, 2003.
———. *Stafford's Mineral Springs and Springs House*. Self-published, 2014.
———. *Stafford Village*. Self-published, 2016.
———. *West Stafford*. Self-published, 2013.
———. *Willington Avenue*. Self-published, 2010.
History of the Town of Stafford. Stafford, CT: Stafford Library Association, 1935.
McDermott, William P. *The American Dream: Yankees, Irish, and Canadians in 19th Century Connecticut*. Tolland, CT: Kerleen Press, 2012.
———. *Stafford, Connecticut, 1719–1870: From Farm to Factory*. Tolland, CT: Kerleen Press, 2010.
1776–1976: Stafford Historical Highlights. Ellington, CT: K&R Printers.
Stafford, Connecticut: 250th Anniversary. Stafford, CT: Town of Stafford 250th Anniversary Committee, 1969.
Stafford Historical Society. *Historical Vignettes Volume 1: Stafford Connecticut 275th Anniversary 1719–1994*. Stafford Springs, CT: LiDasigns Printers, 1994.
Witt, Earl M. *A History of the Schools of Stafford, Connecticut*. Stafford, CT: Stafford Teachers' Club, 1946.
———. *150 Years of Methodism in Stafford Springs*. Stafford Springs, CT: 1980.
Young, William. *Stafford Illustrated: A Descriptive and Historical Sketch of Stafford Connecticut*. Stafford, CT: Young & Cady Publishers, 1895.

About the Stafford Historical Society

The Stafford Historical Society was founded in 1962 by a group of local citizens who were interested in preserving Stafford's history. The museum, located at 5 Spring Street in Stafford Springs, was built in 1889 as the office and display rooms of local businessman Julius Converse. The famed Stafford Springs Mineral Water was bottled in the basement. It later became the home of the Stafford Public Library for more than 100 years.

The museum features numerous exhibits of local artifacts, as well as a research library containing an extensive collection of books, newspapers, photographs, postcards, and various other items of local interest. The society also shares many of its photographs, announces and publicizes programs and events, and maintains contact with the community through its Facebook page.

The Stafford Historical Society holds several meetings throughout the year, each followed by an informative program of historical interest. All programs are open to the public at no charge. Anyone with an interest in the history of Stafford is encouraged to attend and to consider joining the Stafford Historical Society to assist with the mission of preserving Stafford's history.

DISCOVER THOUSANDS OF LOCAL HISTORY BOOKS FEATURING MILLIONS OF VINTAGE IMAGES

Arcadia Publishing, the leading local history publisher in the United States, is committed to making history accessible and meaningful through publishing books that celebrate and preserve the heritage of America's people and places.

Find more books like this at
www.arcadiapublishing.com

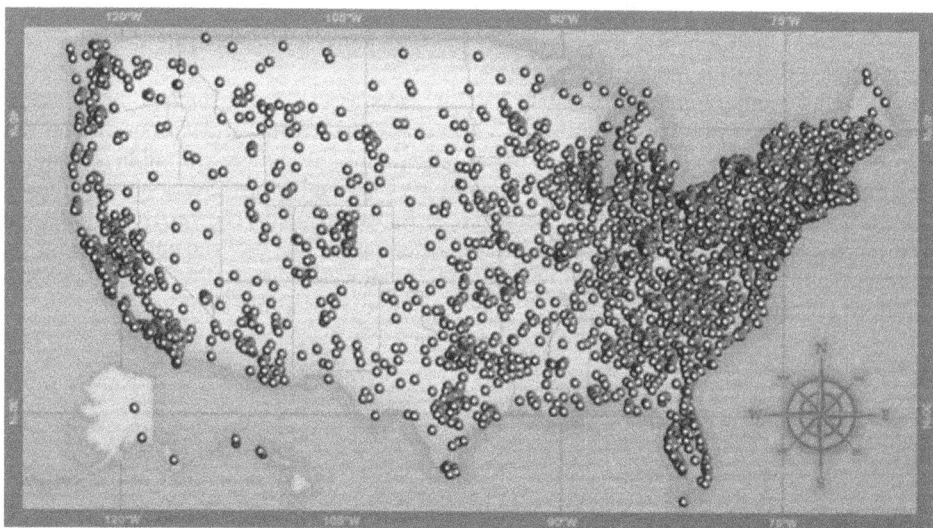

Search for your hometown history, your old stomping grounds, and even your favorite sports team.

www.ingramcontent.com/pod-product-compliance
Lightning Source LLC
Chambersburg PA
CBHW080908100426
42812CB00007B/2209